ARKANA

W9-DAB-905

Gurdjieff

An Approach to His Ideas

Michel Waldberg

Gurdjieff
An Approach to His Ideas

Translated by Steve Cox

ARKANA

ARKANA

Published by the Penguin Group
27 Wrights Lane, London W8 5TZ, England
Viking Penguin Inc., 40 West 23rd Street, New York, New York 10010, USA
Penguin Books Australia Ltd, Ringwood, Victoria, Australia
Penguin Books Canada Ltd, 2801 John Street, Markham, Ontario, Canada L3R 1B4
Penguin Books (NZ) Ltd, 182–190 Wairau Road, Auckland 10, New Zealand

Penguin Books Ltd, Registered Offices: Harmondsworth, Middlesex, England

Originally published in French as *Gurdjieff* by Editions Seghers 1973
This English translation first published by Routledge & Kegan Paul Ltd 1981
Published by Arkana 1989
10 9 8 7 6 5 4 3 2 1

Printed and bound in Great Britain by
Cox & Wyman Ltd, Reading
Set in Baskerville

Contents

Foreword

The elaborate system of thought, behavior, psychological development, taught by Gurdjieff and his chief disciple, Ouspensky, was
often called by them and their pupils the work. . . . It insists upon
men making unwearied efforts to free themselves from a waking
sleep or being mere machines, to become fully conscious, to build
up a central commanding 'I' in place of a score of contradictory
'I's', to rid themselves of wasteful and stupid negative emotions,
to make 'essence' grow at the expense of false 'personality', and
not to imagine they are in easy possession of immortal souls but to
believe that in the end, after unremittent effort, they might create
in themselves such an indestructible soul.

It is surprising how little public attention has been given to the
work. A good deal has been written about it from the inside – I
must possess at least twenty of such books myself – but, so far as I
know, nothing of importance from the outside. If a disinterested
critical examination of Gurdjieff's teaching and ideas exists it has
never come my way.

These words were written by J. B. Priestley in 1964 in his book *Man
and Time* (London, Aldus Books in conjunction with W. H. Allen &
Son). Now, nearly twenty years later, just such a disinterested and
critical appraisal of Gurdjieff's teaching is to be found in Michel
Waldberg's book.

Priestley singles out two early students of these ideas: A. R.
Orage, 'once the most brilliant editor in Britain', and Maurice
Nicoll, 'a pupil of Jung and then a distinguished Harley Street
specialist'. He then goes on to say, 'The level of Gurdjieff's and

Ouspensky's most devoted students was very high. In order to study this movement nobody will have to do any intellectual slumming.'

(Priestley also describes the teaching of Gurdjieff as 'in fact a kind of esoteric Christianity' and recommends 'readers interested in this aspect to look at Maurice Nicoll's *The New Man* and *The Mark* in which he re-interprets the Gospels'.)

Another pupil of Gurdjieff's was Kenneth Walker, the eminent surgeon, colleague and friend of Maurice Nicoll. The following passage taken from his book *A Study of Gurdjieff's Teaching* (published in 1957) is still fresh and relevant because it draws attention to the difficulties inherent in any attempt to convey certain dimensions of experience and insight by means of the written word:

> It is because Gurdjieff's teaching possesses the qualities of coherence, integration and growth, characteristic of life, that I am attempting to bring it to the notice of other people, so far as it is possible to do this in a book. This last conditional clause is necessary, for formulation and printing squeeze out of the spoken word almost all of its vitality, as pressing deprives a flower of nearly all its beauty. . . . Unfortunately there is no way of avoiding the devitalizing effect of books on oral teaching, and all that can be done in the present instance is to warn the reader that it is bound to happen. . . .
>
> The Zen Buddhist Master likens all teaching to the pointing of a finger at the moon, and his disciple is very severely repri-manded if he places emphasis on the finger instead of the object at which the finger is pointing. So also must Gurdjieff's teaching be looked upon as a finger which directs attention to certain principles and methods which, properly used, can lead to certain results. . . . Gurdjieff did not draw diagrams on a board and teach from these. His method of instruction was far less comfortable for his class than this. He carved out from us living chunks of experience and taught from them. One found one's own petty vanities and follies being used as specimens on which Gurdjieff was able to demonstrate to his class the mechanical nature of human life. A book is but a poor sub-stitute for such vital and direct teaching as this.

Elsewhere (*Venture With Ideas*, London, Jonathan Cape, 1951) Kenneth Walker was able to give his personal impression of Gurdjieff the man:

It would be fitting to insert here a picture of the man . . . Gurdjieff. Fitting, yes, but as difficult a task as to paint a portrait of that old Sea-God Proteus, 'who knew everything and was capable of assuming any shape'. Gurdjieff had Proteus's many-sidedness. . . . He could create any impression he liked and would often supply whatever his visitors expected of him. . . . It was not part of his work to disarm hostility and to make converts, but to give help to those who had already dis-covered that they were in need of help. . . .

Everything Gurdjieff did seemed to originate from within. . . . He never fumbled in his thought or his movements. The latter were always purposeful and made with the strictest economy of effort, like those of a cat, and his immense capacity for work was due to this ability of his never to waste energy. The more I saw of Gurdjieff the more convinced I became of his uniqueness. He had qualities which I had never seen in anybody else; profound knowledge, immense vitality and complete immunity from fear. Gurdjieff once said: 'I have very good leather to sell to those who want to make shoes out of it'.

No better description than this could be given to Gurdjieff's role as a teacher. He was a man who had ideas of an extraordinarily high quality to sell to those who required ideas of this kind. More-over, he had used the word 'sell' deliberately because he always maintained that men never appreciated anything which they had not paid for; the payment need not necessarily be in terms of money, but something had to have been sacrificed if the leather they had acquired was to be properly appreciated. . . . The buyer would have to make something out of the leather he had bought, and nothing could be more serviceable than a strong pair of shoes for life's difficult journey.

Michel Waldberg's own warm appreciation of Gurdjieff is evident throughout his book, distilled as it inevitably had to be from less direct sources. The author's evaluation of Gurdjieff's extraordinary book *Beelzebub's Tales to His Grandson* is considerable and construc-tive and forms a large part of his book, together with his own outline of the principal ideas of the teaching.

A. R. Orage, whose influence pervaded so much of the best thought and literature in England during the first thirty years of this century, was also one of the pupils who helped to translate *Beelze-*

bub's Tales to His Grandson into English. It is fortunate that he left his own observations about this book and its author so that we can draw upon his testimony (see C. S. Nott, *Teachings of Gurdjieff*):

> Beelzebub's Tales is a book that destroys existing values; it compels the serious reader to re-value all values, and, to a sincere person, it is devastating. As Gurdjieff says, it may destroy your relish for your favourite dish.

> Every 'three-brained being' at a certain stage . . . asks himself 'What is the meaning and the aim of existence? What am I here for? Why was I born? How did I come to be born in this particular family, in these conditions? What must I do?'
> Beelzebub tells his grandson, Hassein, not to think about it too much yet. He is still young and must study. . . . For the keys to the answers are all there, though, as Gurdjieff says, they are not near the doors.

> Consider the epic quality of the setting of the story. It is a kind of dialogue between Beelzebub, an actualized, ideal, objectively conscious man . . . who is stating his conclusions, impartially, constructively, to a young undeveloped being who has a longing to understand. Beelzebub surveys and observes the body of the cosmos. . . . He implies that the universe has a purpose, and that he understands it. Solar systems, planets, beings, the life of man, all organic life, has a practical, not a theoretical, or mystical function; and the various parts of the megalocosmos, including us men, either fulfil, or do not fulfil, their function.
> Beelzebub has made use of his exile to lead a conscious existence and has spared no effort to actualize his potentialities. He is what we might be. He is what we ought to be.

We can receive an impression of Gurdjieff of a different order if we refer to Thomas de Hartmann's book *Our Life with Mr. Gurdjieff*. De Hartmann was primarily a musician: his life in Russia prior to the Revolution was lived in the higher echelons of the society of that day, which included service in the Guards. We owe to him the complete compositions surrounding the musical themes suggested by Gurdjieff, as recounted in Ouspensky's *In Search of the Miraculous*. De Hartmann himself was a man of brilliant technical achievement in the world of music in Tsarist Russia, but in spite of the rigidity of his early years he was able, due to his essential simplicity, to journey with Gurdjieff through the Caucasus and finally to Constantinople, passing through the maze of the conflicting aspects of the Bolshevik Revolution. Some passages from his book illustrate the directness and personal nature of Gurdjieff's teaching:

> Mr. Gurdjieff demanded of us a very great effort, especially difficult because we did not know when it would end. We suffered and would have been only too happy to rest, but there was no protest in us, because the one thing we really wished was to follow Mr. Gurdjieff. Everything else seemed unimportant beside that.
>
> He told about the aim and methods of work and the day when he hoped to open the Institute. Then he asked us: 'What name would you give such an Institute?' We tried to think of a name that would connect with all that Mr. Gurdjieff had just told us. He rejected every suggestion. Finally, as if we had been squeezing our brains like a tube of tooth-paste, the word 'harmonious' came out.
>
> Afterwards it was clear to me that Mr. Gurdjieff had decided on this name some time earlier, but instead of giving us a ready-made word, he forced us to look for it, pushed us, tried to bring us closer to the main thought, till this word emerged. Finally we had the name for the Institute which Mr. Gurdjieff wished. It was 'The Institute for the Harmonious Development of Man'.

Michel Waldberg's book is an honest and serious study of the principles of Gurdjieff's teaching. But bearing in mind that traditionally a teaching is transmitted directly from master to pupil, let us conclude with a passage from the Translators' Note to the second series of Gurdjieff's writings, *Meetings with Remarkable Men*:

> Gurdjieff was a master.
>
> According to traditional conceptions, the function of a master is not limited to the teaching of doctrines, but implies an actual incarnation of knowledge, thanks to which he can awaken other men, and help them in their search simply by his presence.

Acknowledgments

Grateful acknowledgment is made to the following copyright owners and publishers for their kind permission to reprint extracts from their works: The Estate of Kenneth Walker and Jonathan Cape Ltd for extracts from *A Study of Gurdjieff's Teaching* and *Venture with Ideas*; E. P. Dutton and Routledge & Kegan Paul for extracts from *Beelzebub's Tales to his Grandson* and *Meetings with Remarkable Men* by G. I Gurdjieff; Harcourt Brace Jovanovich Inc. and Routledge & Kegan Paul for extracts from *In Search of the Miraculous* by P. D. Ouspensky (copyright 1949 by Harcourt Brace Jovanovich Inc. renewed 1977 by Tatiana Nagro).

1 Reflections on the 'inhumanity' of Gurdjieff

The name of Gurdjieff almost always arouses suspicion or hostility. The man is usually described as a kind of werewolf or cynical tyrant, demanding much from others and little from himself, making use of his disciples for mysterious ends, seeking powers rather than virtue, and with an absolute contempt for the whole of humanity.

As for his teaching, it is supposed to be impenetrable, arid and deadening, because it contains a ruthless, 'objectively impartial' critique of human life. Because that critique is ferociously funny; because it is radical, and nothing which constitutes the human treasure escapes it; because in an allegedly Christian civilization Gurdjieff condemns the sophism whereby inconsistency is forgiven in the name of mercy; because he reminds us, as do all the great masters, of primary truths, and tells us that a Christian 'is not a man who calls himself a Christian or whom others call a Christian – Christian is one who lives in accordance with Christ's precepts';[1] because the way he proposes, which is the way of *consciousness*, appears arrogant to the ordinary eye, and because he is blamed for not giving love its place.

So Gurdjieff is seen as an 'inhuman' figure, demonstrating what he calls 'the Terror of the Situation', and offering a 'dry' path to his disciples. Whereas the humane master is supposed to be understanding and compassionate, gentle and benevolent.

But it must be emphasized that ordinary language is quite mistaken when it associates the notions of benevolence or compassion with the notion of sweetness. Gurdjieff is less isolated than is commonly believed when he rejects common paths, received ideas, and morality in the ordinary sense of the word; when he rails against men; and when, in order to work on men's minds effectively, he employs humour and bad taste, the 'way of blame'. No matter what has been said about him, benevolence, compassion and – above all – goodness are qualities which he developed in himself to the highest degree, while never allowing them to be associated with any useless and harmful gentleness.

It is in the apparently brutal relationship with a disciple that these qualities are manifested. For to love the disciple means not to console but to heal him. And the more serious the disease, the more violent the cure. Sometimes, in fact, amputation is necessary. 'If thy right eye offend thee,' said Christ, 'pluck it out, and cast it from thee.'[2]

But Gurdjieff is not only a doctor, or a surgeon. He also points men towards paths to wisdom and happiness. Painful paths, often arduous, barren paths in the eyes of those whose 'personality' (that rigid monster) lacks the necessary flexibility to overcome obstacles; but they are also straighter ways, for those whose hearts are not yet hardened, for those 'common men' who have not systematically 'wiseacred', but have listened humbly and attentively to the 'inner voice'. For apart from the rugged path of the School, there exists the way of life, of 'popular' wisdom whose importance Gurdjieff always stressed. Thus in the first chapter of *Beelzebub's Tales* he writes: 'I [am] a follower in general not only of the theoretical – as contemporary people have become – but also of the practical sayings of popular wisdom which have become fixed by the centuries.'[3]

This special way is the way of the *obyvatel*. '*Obyvatel* is a strange word in the Russian language,' Gurdjieff said. 'It is used in the sense of "inhabitant", without any particular shade. At the same time it is used to express contempt or derision – "*obyvatel*" – as though there could be nothing worse. But those who speak in this way do not understand that the *obyvatel* is the healthy kernel of life.'[4]

It is also along the way of the *obyvatel* that the traveller encounters the legendary Persian master Mullah Nassr Eddin (Nasrudin), whom Gurdjieff constantly mentions in his books, ascribing to him most popular aphorisms and the most baffling and the wisest of his commentaries.

There exists in the Islamic world a legend of Mullah Nassr Eddin, a body of anecdotes whose hero is a master of paradox. For the Mullah is both the wisest of initiates and, apparently, the most stupid of yokels. Whether the Mullah really existed does not matter. He is the hero of hundreds of good stories which are also superb fables, some of which can rival the best of the many Zen stories collected by D. T. Suzuki in his *Essays*.

Several of these stories appear, with shrewd commentaries by Idries Shah, in his book *The Sufis*.[5] The following is among the most typical:

> The Mullah was thinking aloud.
> 'How do I know whether I am dead or alive?'
> 'Don't be such a fool,' his wife said; 'if you were dead your limbs would be cold.'
> Shortly afterwards Nasrudin was in the forest cutting wood. It was midwinter. Suddenly he realized that his hands and feet were cold.
> 'I am undoubtedly dead,' he thought; 'so I must stop working, because corpses do not work.'
> And, because corpses do not walk about, he lay down on the grass.
> Soon a pack of wolves appeared and started to attack Nasrudin's donkey, which was tethered to a tree.
> 'Yes, carry on, take advantage of a dead man,' said Nasrudin from his prone position; 'but if I had been alive I would not have allowed you to take liberties with my donkey.'

In *Beelzebub's Tales*, as well as in *Meetings With Remarkable Men*, Mullah Nassr Eddin is constantly intervening, either to pronounce one of those 'true and scathing' sentences from his inexhaustible store, or to comment in a few words on a situation which Gurdjieff sees as characteristic of the inconsistency of human beings.

Mullah Nassr Eddin makes his appearance in order to remind us of the limits of the intellect; unless the whole being is involved, experience is in vain, and knowledge evanescent. The Mullah reaches his ends by apparently improbable means. He is the master of the way of blame, where the initiator takes on the role of the fool, the idiot, or the madman. But predicaments, however tricky they may be, always turn to his advantage.

Another master of the way of blame was Christ. Now we live in a society which is dominated, consciously or unconsciously, by the image of 'gentle Jesus'. When Gurdjieff affirms that we are suffering from 'the crystallization of the consequences of the properties of the maleficent organ Kundabuffer', an organ which causes us to per-ceive reality upside-down, I can think of no better justification of this admirable myth than the expression 'gentle Jesus' applied to the man who said: 'Think not that I am come to send peace on earth: I came not to send peace, but a sword.'[6] Nobody would dream of calling Christ inhuman.

Gurdjieff is often reproached for the way he rebuffed the curious and refused to answer any of their questions. But this same 'gentle Jesus' said: 'Give not that which is holy unto the dogs, neither cast ye your pearls before swine, lest they trample them under their feet, and turn again and rend you.'[7]

Something else needs pointing out here, and that is that we find Gurdjieff all the harder to swallow because he addresses us in our own language, tells us in our own language: Become aware of your own nothingness. If he had been a Zen master, for instance, we would find him infinitely easier to accept. Yet anyone who has read Suzuki's *Essays in Zen Buddhism* knows how much violence may enter into the relations between master and disciple at the very core of Zen. But Zen is fashionable. Hence it is acceptable for a master to call his disciple a 'rice-bag', or take a stick to him, or slap him: it's exotic. Or else, worse still, Zen is watered down as Christianity has been watered down. The only thing that matters in Zen is the bliss of *satori*. The incredible efforts made by disciples to attain it are forgotten. In the end we come to confuse this or that rare emotion with true *satori*.

Gurdjieff, knowing the way people's minds work, protected himself against such abuses. He piled up the obstacles, highlighted the difficulties, demanded much of those who wanted to follow him. He spewed out the lukewarm, and for this they never forgave him.

2   The 'way of blame'

Gurdjieff tells us, 'Men are not men.' A scandalous remark, if ever
there was one, for we have never questioned our own humanity. We
have described it as sinful, of course, but we have always thought
that, however serious our weaknesses might be, we could become
aware of them and take steps to correct them. Gurdjieff denies us the
capacity to understand and to do just that. We have never really
believed in the 'terror of the situation', considering the norm as
accidental. But the norm is folly and impotence. We think that these
are fortuitous, and that, taking the good years with the bad, mankind is making progress – that war, for example, is an exceptional
phenomenon. And when a master appears who tells us that most
men are irresponsible machines, totally subject to their own automatic behaviour, incapable of developing even the embryo of a soul,
we react indignantly. Because statements like that destroy the
humanist ideas that we have always fostered, no matter how
pessimistic we may be. The fact is that we have not heard the lesson
of the masters.

   We have not listened to Chateaubriand, or Balzac, or Baudelaire,
or Lautréamont, or Rimbaud, to name but a few. We have not taken
Breton's warning cry really seriously. We may have loved these
authors with a sentimental love, admiring them for the beauty of
their style or the nobility of their bearing, but we have not heard
them.

   Gurdjieff is only saying what they have said already:

      Folly and error, avarice and vice,
      Employ our souls and waste our bodies' force.

As mangy beggars incubate their lice,
We nourish our innocuous remorse.

Our sins are stubborn, craven our repentance.
For our weak vows we ask excessive prices.
Trusting our tears will wash away the sentence,
We sneak off where the muddy road entices.

These are the opening lines of *Les Fleurs du Mal*.[1]

And we should also listen to Lautréamont: 'Throughout my life I have seen, without one exception, narrow-shouldered men performing innumerable idiotic acts, brutalising their fellows and corrupting souls by every means. The motive for their actions they call *Glory*.'[2]

Or then again there is Rimbaud's cry:

If old imbeciles had not found nothing but the false meaning of the I, we would not have to sweep away those millions of skeletons which have everlastingly hoarded up the products of their one-eyed intellect, while claiming to be its authors![3]

Baudelaire again, in his private diary, wrote:

It is impossible to read through any newspaper, any day, any month, or any year, without finding on every line the more frightful signs of human perversity, alongside the most astounding boasts of integrity, goodness and charity, and the most brazen declarations concerning progress and civilization.

All newspapers from the first line to the last are nothing but a tissue of horrors. Wars, crimes, thefts, indecencies, tortures, the crimes of princes, the crimes of nations, the crimes of individuals, a frenzy of universal atrocity.

And it is with this disgusting aperitif that the civilized man accompanies his breakfast every morning. Everything in this world reeks of crime: the newspaper, the walls and the face of man.

I do not understand how a pure hand can touch a newspaper without a spasm of disgust.[4]

The poets, that is to say the seers, the clear-sighted, have not deceived themselves, not lulled themselves with the deadly illusion of progress. But they have died of it. They have died of that hunger, that thirst, without which Gurdjieff tells us that no one can find the way. They have died murdered by those monsters of pride and callousness who do not know, or who deny, the existence of the way, being convinced that they already have a soul which only needs a semblance of morality and ritual to acquire blessed immortality.

Gurdjieff is saying the same as the poets, and does not differ from them in his description of 'the three-brained beings of the planet Earth':

'As regards their general psyche itself and its fundamental traits, no matter upon what part of the surface of their planet they arise, these traits in all of them have precisely the same particularities, among them being also that property of the three-brained beings there, thanks to which on that strange planet alone in the whole of the Universe does that horrible process occur among three-brained beings which is called the "process of the destruction of each other's existence," or, as it is called on that ill-fated planet, "war."

'Besides this chief particularity of their common psyche, there are completely crystallized in them and there unfailingly become a part of their common presences – regardless of where they may arise and exist – functions which exist under the names "egoism," "self-love," "vanity," "pride," "self-conceit," "credulity," "suggestibility," and many other properties quite abnormal and quite unbecoming to the essence of any three-brained beings whatsoever.'[5]

Thus mankind is unworthy, and can only gain its freedom if it becomes conscious of its own unworthiness:

Individuality, a single and permanent I, consciousness, will, the *ability to do*, a state of inner freedom, all these are qualities which ordinary man does not possess. . . . He must realize that *he does not exist*; he must realize that he can lose nothing because he has nothing to lose; he must realize his 'nothingness' in the full sense of the term.[6]

In Gurdjieff's teaching, this is the fundamental lesson, the prerequisite for all serious work in the spiritual field. But how do you make men aware of their monstrosity? And what weapons require polishing in order to wake them from the presumptuous sleep which they call their life?

The supreme weapon in this duel of consciousness against sleep is humour, with its corollary, bad taste. The humour in which Freud found 'not only something liberating but also something sublime and elevated'. The humour which Breton described as 'black', which he took care to dissociate from 'silliness, sceptical irony, pleasantry without gravity', and which at its highest is 'the mortal enemy of sentimentality'.[7]

For this is where the shoe pinches. We have an automatic tendency to spontaneously lump ideas together when, not only is their connection unproven, but there are any number of arguments for keeping them apart. Thus for us science, philosophy, theology, mysticism – in other words the quest for truth – are activities which constantly require our utmost seriousness. But are we sure that this word is correctly defined? Certainly 'serious' means 'deserving of consideration', but another of its accepted meanings is 'constituting a danger or threat'. It seems to me that this kind of confusion is revealing, and that there is something equally significant about phrases such as 'serious as the grave', 'a serious contender', 'serious interest'.

There is a confusion between seriousness and gravity, a confusion which Breton exposed and which Gurdjieff made clear. We do not imagine the scholar, the philosopher, the theologian or the mystic roaring with laughter. We say of a moralist that he is grave, and apply the same word to an illness.

When people went to Gurdjieff to ask him a question, only to have him answer not with the desired solemnity but with some disconcerting, irksome rejoinder, and an attitude seemingly inconsequential, perhaps even to the point of being improper or outrageous, then their reasoning followed this sort of course: Gurdjieff is not serious; but a genuine spiritual master is necessarily a serious person; therefore Gurdjieff is not a genuine spiritual master.

But in that case neither would the Zen masters deserve that title, with their theory of laughter, shouts, and blows:

> One evening Yao-shan climbed the mountain for a walk. Seeing the moon suddenly appearing from behind the clouds he laughed most heartily. The laugh echoed ninety *li* east of Li-yang where his monastery was. The villagers thought the voice came from their neighbours. In the morning the inquiry went eastwards from one door to another until it reached the monastery, and the villagers concluded, 'Last night the master gave us the greatest laugh of his life at the top of the mountain.'[8]

Among writers, I believe that it was André Breton who first set out to restore to humour its true life-giving function:

It is less and less certain, seeing the specific demands of modern sensibility, that poetic, artistic, and scientific works and philosophical and social systems lacking in *this sort* of humour do not leave something gravely to be desired, and are not doomed to a more or less rapid death. . . . We are touching upon a burning subject, we are advancing straight into the firing line; we have all the winds of passion alternatively for and against us as soon as we think of lifting the veil from this humour, whose manifest products we nevertheless manage to isolate, with a unique satisfaction, in literature, in art and in life.[9]

This text may illuminate Gurdjieff's behaviour, which was calculated to get rid of a good deal of ill-founded reticence and dissipate a good many misplaced modesties. In particular, *Beelzebub's Tales to His Grandson*, which is often reckoned to be so unapproachable, gains a lot from being understood, not in the way the reader usually attempts to understand a didactic text, but as one of the most perfect expressions of an art form addressed not only to the mind but to the heart and the body too, and which produces that 'explosive' effect without which, as Baudelaire stressed and as Breton reminds us, there can be nothing genuinely comic.

The truly comic is what Baudelaire called the 'absolute comic', which, as he said, is vertigo.[10] A vertigo produced in the *Tales* by the dizzy heights, of men's stupidity or corruption. To describe things otherwise would amount to a death of the mind.

One of the unique virtues of Gurdjieff's books is that they establish a distance between the reader and all that is banal and ordinary, and show us that the banal and ordinary are horrible, because they are actually deeply *foreign* to us. Under the effect of this prose the reader cannot but be bewildered.

To bewilder, baffle and disorientate are the paramount actions of the master. The fact is that we are lost in hostile country, taking the wrong road, and travelling in false dawns.

Gurdjieff said to Ouspensky: 'Awakening begins when a man realizes that he is going nowhere and does not know where to go.'[11] The master is the awakener, and his most effective weapons can be humour and vulgarity.

A brutal intervention from the master is a necessity, otherwise man lulls his consciousness to sleep on the waves of daily life. To be convinced of this, one only needs to reflect upon the meaning of a word like 'disillusionment'. 'Loss of an illusion', the dictionaries say, and this ought to be something positive and reassuring, to anyone claiming to be searching for truth. But evidently not, for the analogous words are heartbreak, letdown, disappointment, disenchantment. Man is too attached to his own errors to enjoy having them pointed out to him.

And that is why the master so often has to take the way of blame, outrage, paradox, contradiction and outward folly. For what is wisdom in the eyes of God is unreason in the eyes of men. What is true in the spiritual order is absurd in the social order. Again, I would like to illustrate this fact with the help of two anecdotes whose hero is that master of the way of blame, the legendary Mullah Nassr Eddin.

It is noon, and a blazing hot day. In the village square the perspiring Mullah, covered in dust, is down on all fours looking for something in the sand.

One of his neighbours sees him, comes up and asks:

'What have you lost?'

'My key,' says the Mullah, who goes on scrabbling in the sand while his neighbour squats down to help him look.

After a few minutes the sweating, panting neighbour asks:

'Are you sure it was here that you lost it?'

'No,' says the Mullah, 'it was at home.'

'Then why are you looking for it here?'

'My dear fellow, because there's more light here.'

The stories about Mullah Nassr Eddin, besides being 'funny', also have a 'metaphysical' value; they are worrying and disturbing. Gurdjieff delighted in telling them, and even in making them up. Mullah Nassr Eddin, often the embodiment of popular wisdom, assumes above all the role of the fool whose apparently absurd logic turns conventional ideas upside-down.

Another day, the Mullah goes into a shop, and the shopkeeper comes forward to serve him.

'First things first,' says the Mullah. 'Are you sure you saw me enter your shop?'

'Of course I am!'

'Have you met me before?'

'Never.'

'Then how do you know it's me?'

These anecdotes are a triumph of vulgarity: in them everything that 'goes without saying' is radically put in question.

Gurdjieff often behaved like the Mullah. One of his disciples writes:

> For example, he never hesitated to arouse doubts about himself by the kind of language he used, by his calculated contradictions and by his behaviour, to such a point that people around him, particularly those who had a tendency to worship him blindly, were finally obliged to open their eyes to the chaos of their reactions.[12]

On the way of blame the initiator can appear brutal, incoherent, and outrageous.

The master is first of all the man who knows *me*, who knows *my* need (I myself do not know myself; I do not know what I really need). I am Nathaniel, and the master has seen me under the fig tree. No one but he knows, or will ever know, what happened under that tree.

The master knows me, knows my need, knows the paths that lead to the Good I yearn for. But he cannot simply tell me these things, he can only help me to understand them, 'with all my mass' as Gurdjieff used to say. He cannot explain them to me, he can only indicate them: the finger does not explain the moon, the Zen saying reminds us, but it points to it, and woe betide the man who mistakes the finger for the moon.

How does the master go about demonstrating reality? He resorts to what Zen calls 'skilful means' (*upāyakauśalya*). This means replying to the disciple's questions with raised finger, outstretched arms, threatening stick, shouts and blows. This also means paradoxes, contradictions, repetitions, exclamations, apparently indolent answers or even refusals to reply and many other usually unexpected means:

> When Jōshu was asked by a monk whether there was Buddha-Nature in the dog, the master answered 'Mu!'
> Reiun was asked, 'How were things *before* the appearance of the Buddha in the world?' He raised his hossu.*[13]

---

* Suzuki notes that a 'hossu', part of what he calls 'the various religious insignia' of the Zen master, was 'originally a mosquito driver in India'. (Tr.)

Refusal of the useless question, and behaviour provoking the often painful awakening of the disciple, these are what I see as the essence of this way of blame which I have tried roughly to explain.

But to return to Gurdjieff: he offers his mainly 'intellectual' disciples an exemplarily coherent system whose study should enable them to make real progress. The coherence of this system is seductive, but there is a danger of its discouraging the pupil because of its complexity and the demands which its method imposes. The master who embodies the system seems distant and perhaps inaccessible. But at the same time Gurdjieff lessens this distance by his close relationship with the disciple, by his fatherly attitude and benevolence, although he does not hesitate, if need be, to play the role of the fool, which is the master's role on the way of blame:

> When he assumes this role, the master is a mirror. A mirror in which the disciple sees himself. He caricatures and exaggerates what 'is not working' in the disciple, feigns anger, arrogance, and if necessary lecherousness, and is therefore disconcerting, because the disciple has a long way to go before realizing that the hateful person the master is showing him is himself.[14]

Here is the explanation of many apparent contradictions. All sorts of resentment and bitterness are dispelled when, in the mirror of the master, you see yourself.

In this way Gurdjieff carries out the first of the tasks which he set himself both in his life and in his work, and which he defines as 'To destroy, mercilessly, without any compromises whatsoever, in the mentation and feelings of the reader, the beliefs and views, by centuries rooted in him, about everything existing in the world.'[15]

It is in this sense that he may appear 'inhuman', because his undertaking is anything but 'moral' in the usual sense of the word. He told Ouspensky:

> '*What is necessary is conscience.* We do not teach morality. We teach how to find conscience. People are not pleased when we say this. They say that we have no *love*. Simply because we do not encourage weakness and hypocrisy but, on the contrary, take off all masks.'[16]

3 The 'work' and its aim

Once the disciple has been awakened, how will he make progress along the way of conscience, and then of love? Because the first precedes the second, but the second proceeds from the first.

First, as I say, there is the system, the body of work which constitutes the teachings of Gurdjieff, and which is mainly to be found in the books of Ouspensky and Maurice Nicoll. In addition to a description of man and the universe, and an analysis of the great psychological and cosmic laws, this contains the definition of what Gurdjieff called 'the fourth way', as opposed to the traditional religious ways.

The central idea of the system is ancient and well known: that we must know ourselves, learn to locate ourselves correctly in our 'megalocosmos', and therefore find out how the human machine works and become capable of controlling it. But the method proposed by Gurdjieff to achieve this aim is a new one, at least in the West. I shall further analyse this method later on, but here let me venture to underline some of its strengths.

We are, says Gurdjieff, 'three-brained beings'. This means simply that our nature is threefold. It participates simultaneously in the physical, the emotional, and the mental order. In each of us one of these three orders, one of the three 'centres', dominates the others. There are men of the physical body, men of feeling and men of intellect. According to Gurdjieff's teaching, for each of these types there is a corresponding way. The first is the way of the fakir, or the way of asceticism; the second is the way of the monk, or way of religious feeling; the third is the way of the yogi, or way of reason. The common basis of these ways is religion, in the institutional sense of the word. They are traditional and '*permanent* . . . within the limits of our historical period'.[1] All the spiritual processes we know come down to one of these three ways, according to Gurdjieff.

The way which he himself proposes is that of work on all three centres at the same time. All work on one of the centres must accompany corresponding work on the two others. Under no circumstances should the balance of the centres be broken. It is this work and only this work, says Gurdjieff, which may give us access to conscience:

'Then the fourth way differs from the other ways in that the principal demand made upon a man is the demand for understanding. A man must do nothing that he does not understand, except as an experiment under the supervision and direction of his teacher. The more a man understands what he is doing, the greater will be the results of his efforts. This is a fundamental principle of the fourth way. The results of work are in proportion to the consciousness of the work. No "faith" is required on the fourth way; on the contrary, faith of any kind is opposed to the fourth way. On the fourth way a man must satisfy himself of the truth of what he is told. And until he is satisfied he must do nothing.'[2]

This definition generally outrages people, because it looks as if Gurdjieff's way must by its very nature be accessible only to a chosen few, and because it assumes an immense amount of work on oneself, and seems to give precedence to this task apparently to the detriment of the love of God.

I believe that this fourth way was, quite simply, devised for times in which the very love of which people imagine themselves capable is itself an illusion. This way is – and I insist that the point must be properly understood – the *sine qua non* of love. It excludes love only in so far as that love is debased in human beings:

' "In the presences of the beings of contemporary times, there also arises and is present in them as much as you please of that strange impulse which they call love; but this love of theirs is firstly also the result of certain crystallized consequences of the properties of the same Kundabuffer; and secondly this impulse of theirs arises and manifests itself in the process of every one of them entirely subjectively; so subjectively and so differently that if ten of them were asked to explain how they sensed this inner impulse of theirs, then all ten of them – if, of course, they for once replied sincerely, and frankly confessed their genuine sensations and not those they had read about somewhere or had obtained from somebody else – all ten would reply differently and describe ten different sensations.

'"One would explain this sensation in the sexual sense; another in the sense of pity; a third in the sense of desire for submission; a fourth, in a common craze for outer things, and so on and so forth; but not one of the ten could describe even remotely, the sensation of genuine Love.

'"And none of them would, because in none of the ordinary beings-men here has there ever been for a long time, any sensation of the sacred being-impulse of genuine Love. And without this 'taste' they cannot even vaguely describe that most beatific sacred being-impulse in the presence of every three-centered being of the whole Universe, which, in accordance with the divine foresight of Great Nature, forms those data in us, from the result of the experiencing of which we can blissfully rest from the meritorious labors actualized by us for the purpose of self-perfection."'[3]

Gurdjieff asserts that we are incapable of love, belief or hope in the higher, sublime sense of these words, and that is why the way he proposes appears inhuman to some people.

But work along this way has necessarily to be carried out in a group, and under the guidance of a teacher, and I have shown that the teacher is also the man who knows *me*, who loves me (because he himself is capable of love), and that this bond between teacher and disciple tempers what ever aridity there might be on the way.

Furthermore – and again I must insist on this fact – Gurdjieff does not condemn the traditional ways. He simply points out that in general man does not fully realize himself in them. Also, and this is perhaps the most important point, the system is not everything. The fourth way is not exclusive. It is not the sole way to salvation.

In the end, in fact, the four ways make only a single way. They make what Gurdjieff calls 'the subjective way', although he takes care to add that the word 'subjective' is only an approximation.[4] But there exists another way, which he calls 'the objective way', with the same reservations about the adjective. This is the way I have already mentioned, the way of the *obyvatel*, of the man in the street:

'People of the objective way simply live in life. They are those whom we call good people. Particular systems and methods are not necessary for them; making use of ordinary religious or intellectual teachings and ordinary morality, they live at the same time according to conscience. They do not of necessity do much good, but they do no evil. Sometimes they happen to be quite uneducated, simple people but they understand life very well, they have a right valuation of things and a right outlook. And they are of course perfecting themselves and evolving. Only their way can be very long with many unnecessary repetitions.'[5]

So all is not rotten in our state. If *Beelzebub's Tales* offer us an atrocious image of man, *Meetings With Remarkable Men* is alive with *obyvatels*:

I do not at all wish to say that all *obyvatels* are people of the objective way. Nothing of the kind. Among them are thieves, rascals, and fools; but there are others. I merely wish to say that being a good *obyvatel* by itself does not hinder the 'way'. . . . A man lives and works, then, when his children or his grandchildren are grown up, he gives everything to them and goes into a monastery. This is the *obyvatel* of which I speak. Perhaps he does not go into a monastery, perhaps he does not need this. His own life as an *obyvatel* can be his way.[6]

The chief culprit responsible for the 'terror of the situation' is the intellectual, in the Western sense of the word, symbolized in *Beelzebub's Tales* by the 'subsequent Universal Hasnamuss' Lentrohamsanin. It is he whom Gurdjieff calls in his myth the 'destroyer of the Very Saintly Labors'. It is he who is at the root of that subjectivation of values, done in the name of liberty, which has produced Babel, and the Circle of the Confusion of Tongues, in which we live.

The culprits are the intellectuals, because they are also the teachers. Not only are their own minds distorted, but they also warp the minds of the *obyvatels*, more and more of whom are falling into their clutches. Even so, some of these are 'quite uneducated, simple people' who 'understand life very well' and may escape corruption.

Christ said, a long time ago: 'I thank thee, O Father, Lord of heaven and earth, because thou hast hid these things from the wise and prudent, and hast revealed them unto babes.'[7] For these 'babes' the yoke is easy and the burden light. For us, there is a cross to take up and a tribute of sufferings to pay. Once it has been paid we can gain access to conscience and become capable of love.

Gurdjieff always said this. His work is an exaltation of conscience, a vindication of love.

Two sentences from *Meetings With Remarkable Men* sum up the essence of his teaching to perfection. The first is, '*Only he will deserve the name of man and can count upon anything prepared for him from Above, who has already acquired corresponding data for being able to preserve intact both the wolf and the sheep confided to his care.*'[8] In other words, we must set out to achieve freedom of body, emotions and mind, which are symbolized respectively by the wolf, the lamb and the shepherd. The second sentence recalls the 'very sensible counsel for living often employed by our great Mullah Nassr Eddin'. It runs, 'Always and in everything strive to attain at the same time what is useful for others and what is pleasant for oneself.'[9]

But where is the suffering in that? Suffering is necessary while one is still incapable of being useful to anybody. Suffering is necessary, but we have to learn to renounce our sufferings, and finally to renounce our renunciations.

'I have already said before that sacrifice is necessary,' said G. 'Without sacrifice nothing can be attained. But if there is anything in the world that people do not understand it is the idea of sacrifice. They think they have to sacrifice something that they have. For example, I once said that they must sacrifice "faith," "tranquillity," "health." They understand this literally. But then the point is that they have not got either faith, or tranquillity, or health. All these words must be taken in quotation marks. In actual fact they have to sacrifice only what they imagine they have and which in reality they do not have. They must sacrifice their fantasies. But this is difficult for them, very difficult. It is much easier to sacrifice real things.

'Another thing that people must sacrifice *is their suffering.*'[10]

And Gurdjieff adds: 'No one who is not free from suffering, who has not sacrificed his suffering, can work.'

The ultimate aim of this work is pleasure, which is 'an *attribute of paradise*'. But this pleasure is not accessible 'now, at once and forever'. 'The whole point is to be able to get pleasure and be able to keep it. *Whoever can do this has nothing to learn*' (my italics).[11]

4   Notes On *Beelzebub's Tales*

One of the obstacles encountered by the student of Gurdjieff's teaching is created by the very style of writing that he uses both in *Beelzebub's Tales to His Grandson* and in *Meetings With Remarkable Men*. Yet these works are not at all alike. One is extraordinarily complex and hard to approach; the other is written more simply, almost in a strictly narrative style. But what they both have in common is that Gurdjieff introduces fantastic elements: in the former, extraterrestrial myths and fictions; in the latter, improbably marvellous events, such as the crossing of the Gobi desert on stilts.

The two books were written in Russian. But what is most remarkable is that the translations made of them both in English and in French have such quality that they stand up as exemplary literary creations in both languages. (There are also German translations of these works, but I shall leave it to German speakers to point out their quality.) How is it that these texts never give a hint of translation? It is because they were undertaken by Gurdjieff's very own disciples, and under his direction; they are the work of a *group* which was not in the least pressed for time, and whose sole concern was to communicate to the reader the special quality of a style unmatched, to my knowledge, in this century.

It has often been said that the style of *Beelzebub's Tales* is awkward. That is because we are not accustomed to it, because it runs counter to all the fashions and all the researches outside of which the iron rule holds that there is no possible salvation for a writer.

The essayist Jorge Luis Borges, well known for his paradoxes and fertile and individual ideas, in an essay entitled 'On the superstitious ethic of the reader' written in 1930 and reprinted in French in the collection *Discussion* (Paris, Gallimard, 1966), also stressed what he called 'the indigent condition of our literature, its inability to attract', which underlie what he considers to be a 'superstition about style':

> Those who are affected by this superstition understand by style not the effectiveness or lack of effectiveness of a page but the apparent successes of the writer – his comparisons, his harmony, the episodes of his punctuation and syntax. They are indifferent to personal conviction or emotion; they look for 'techniqueries' (the word is Unamuno's) which will tell them whether or not what is written has the right to please them.[1]

Here we undoubtedly touch upon the most important problem in present-day literature. Form is no longer the servant of the idea (this statement is not to be taken as a profession of faith in classicism: in Lautréamont, for example, there is nothing gratuitous about the extreme 'baroquery' of the form). On the contrary, form exists, so to speak, in and for itself. And the author will reach the point of seeking to achieve nothing less than the dislocation of language, because he no longer has anything more to communicate than his own confusion, when it is not simply the arrogant affirmation of a pernicious capacity for constant so-called 'innovation'. What Mallarmé unquestionably suffered as a kind of martyrdom, the inability to write, which emerges in his work in the double dead-end of unintelligibility and affectation, most of today's writers experience through their own conformism, because it has become 'good taste' to hold forth incessantly about the celebrated 'incommunicability' of just about everything.

Hence the 'superstition about style' so roundly condemned by Borges when he says of writers,

> They have heard it said that close repetition of certain syllables is cacophonous, and they will pretend to be put out by it in prose, even if in poetry it brings them a particular – and in my opinion equally pretended – pleasure. *In other words they are looking not at the efficiency of the machinery but the arrangement of its parts*. They are subordinating emotion to ethic, or rather to good form [my italics].[2]

Writers nearly always look for the 'page of perfection', but, as Borges emphasizes,

The page of perfection, the page where not a word can be altered
without damage, is the most precarious of all. . . . Conversely, the
page which is destined for immortality can go through the furnace
of errata, rough versions, careless readings and lack of understanding without losing its soul in the ordeal.[3]

This is the case with the translations we have of the work of
Gurdjieff, apart from the fact that they are quite untouched by the
'furnace of errata'. What Gurdjieff aims for is efficiency, which is
why he has to create an utterly personal language able to convey
both 'personal conviction' and 'emotion'.

The language of *Beelzebub's Tales to His Grandson* has as yet
received very little worthwhile attention. I believe that Charles
Duits's as yet unpublished study – not an exhaustive study, but
rather thoughts which someone might confide, with no literary
intention, to his diary, or to a friend – is worth quoting at length:

'The great qualities of the introduction to the *Tales* need not be
emphasized. That introduction unarguably constitutes, in its own
right, one of the most striking works of its era, and André Breton
considered printing extracts from it in his *Anthology of Black Humour*.

'But the main text of the book is, to say the least, not easy to
approach. Since it so happens that I have been studying it for years,
it seemed that the best means available to me for honouring
Gurdjieff's memory was to make it easier for the reader to approach
this apparently forbidding text, in so far as this is possible.

'In fact it belongs, as the very title indicates, to one of the best-
known of literary genres, the genre of Montesquieu's *Lettres persanes*
and Voltaire's *L'Ingénu*. Beelzebub, a very kindly old man, has
devoted the greater part of his existence to the inhabitants of the
earth. He has tried his hardest to cure them of the terrible disease
which afflicts them because of the "lack of foresight on the part of
certain Most High, Most Very Saintly Cosmic Individuals". So we
already see the "catch", because this being whose behaviour has
obviously been nothing less than "angelic" is considered by human
beings to be the devil in person. Thus, right from the start, we have a
key: men see the world upside-down – that is their disease. They
take Angels for Devils, and Devils for Angels.

'Clearly, if the genre to which *Beelzebub's Tales* belongs is a classic
one, its teaching – or at any rate one of the teachings expressed in
it – is also thoroughly traditional. Beneath the humorous surface of

the fable we again meet the doctrine of illusion, of *Maya*, of the famous "sleep" which all the masters speak off, a sleep which must be broken and, from which the sleeper must "awaken".

'It will also be seen that Gurdjieff is seeking nothing less than to do something "new" – in which respect he certainly distinguishes himself from most professional writers. What is new – and prodigiously so – is the *form*: we have already seen enough to show that the content is ancient, classical and traditional.

'Having said that, it must also be said that no matter how apparently strange, baroque and even preposterous is the form adopted by Gurdjieff to express this traditional thinking, it too belongs to a very old tradition, that of the *Thousand and One Nights*. It seems to me very important to underline this point, because it is indisputable that only a reader capable of taking a *childish* pleasure from listening to stories can appreciate such a work. The gravest problems are at issue, yet Beelzebub is addressing a child, his grandson Hassein, and he narrates the cosmic adventure in the oriental style, that is to say, according to a certain rhythm which has admittedly become quite foreign to the modern Western mind. It is obvious that Homer's listeners enjoyed hearing the same epithets and the same phrases repeated again and again. The same goes for the Sultan listening to Scheherazade, and certainly too for the troubadours' listeners as they learned, for the thousandth time, that Charlemagne had a "flowing beard".

'Here we may be touching on what most deters the modern reader. What for a "childish" mind constitutes the charm and strength of the *Tales* – as of the *Iliad*, the *Chanson de Roland* and the *Thousand and One Nights* – namely the constant harping on the same images, the same expressions, and that tide-like ebb and flow – is just what the "intellectualized" reader finds hardest to take.

'We have to make up our minds here: this is a "process", very different from current practice, and like any other process it has its pros and cons. The use of a "primitive technique" in the twentieth century is obviously a gamble. Most readers will undoubtedly be put off. But some may find something of the fairy tale in them, and also – why mince words? – an inspiration which will carry them along in the end, if they can get over their initial bias.

'The process in question – as anyone soon realizes who has the patience to read a work like the *Tales* – in fact has a very special quality. Certainly a fearsome dragon stands on the threshold of such a book, a dragon which can only be called boredom. But whoever crosses the threshold discovers little by little that the repetitions and so on produce an altogether different effect. They take hold of the reader, create an "atmosphere"; he wants to go further, and like Hassein he asks for more. . . .

'I have mentioned the *Iliad* and the *Thousand and One Nights*; in many ways the *Tales* are also reminiscent of Rabelais, who, like Gurdjieff, takes his time and presents the modern reader with what is at first a hard surface to penetrate, but eventually gains a lasting hold on him. One returns to these books again and again, reading a page, or a chapter, stopping and then starting again, so that their quintessence penetrates without being noticed.

'I have dwelt on the Gurdjieffian process at some length, because it seems to me that what matters most is to prepare the possible reader. Misunderstanding is inevitable if you try to read the *Tales* as you read a novel. There is another way of reading, and therefore another way of considering literature (Joyce also tried to retrieve it in *Ulysses*, and above all in *Finnegans Wake*). A work which has no beginning and no end, which speaks of "all and everything", refuses to make any haste at all, and imposes its own pace on the reader.

'Having said this, we can now tackle the modern and even ultra-modern aspect of the book, Gurdjieff's great comic innovation, an invention which to my mind makes him one of the literary geniuses of the century, and from which he draws an infinite variety of effects whose humour is sometimes disquieting. The entire book is written in a pseudo-scientific jargon whose cumulative effect – but with Gurdjieff all the effects are cumulative – is in my opinion utterly irresistible.

'In some respects the *Tales* are nothing other than a marvellously extended satire on modern science, or to be more precise, on the scientific mind. Certainly Gurdjieff sees the extraordinary vanity of scholars as one of the most perfect illustrations of universal folly. This vanity goes hand in hand with pedantry, and is principally manifested in the continual use of a Greco-Latin jargon which enables the pundits to conceal the ordinariness of what they are saying, exactly like Molière's doctors, and to impose on everyone's credulity. Thus "saliakooríapa" is used for "water", "teskooano" for telescope, etc. I must add straight away that this jargon also has another totally serious purpose: there is in Gurdjieff a "verbal cabbala" which calls for an extremely meticulous and careful examination. But what concerns us here is to see how, with the help of this very simple means, Gurdjieff achieves an effect of absolute disorientation. Beelzebub talks to his grandson Hassein, and of course he talks in his grandson's language. They live on a planet unknown to the men of earth, called Karatas. So that in order to make himself understood by human beings Beelzebub has to *translate* certain of the words he uses. He gravely teaches Hassein the earthmen's word for "saliakooríapa", "teskooano", etc. The reader quickly reaches the point of considering the earth words from the viewpoint of the inhabitants of Karatas, and seriously follows such remarks as:

'And thus the three-brained beings breeding on the planet Earth call the greatest period of the flow of time "century," and this "century" of theirs consists of a hundred "years."
    'A "year" has twelve "months."
    'A "month" has an average of thirty "days," that is, diurnities.
    'Further, they divide their diurnity into twenty-four "hours" and an "hour" into sixty "minutes."
    'And a "minute" they divide into sixty "seconds." '[4]

'. . . only to suddenly be brought up short and then to roar with laughter. For actually he has just learned . . . nothing whatsoever.

'And yet he has after all learned something, for he has begun to consider mankind from outside, and from much further outside than when he slipped into the skin of Montesquieu's Persians or Voltaire's Ingénu. It is our whole language, and hence our whole world, which loses its familiarity, and no longer just various manners, customs, laws and conventions. Like Montesquieu, and like Voltaire, Gurdjieff interposes a distance between the reader and mankind. But here the process is radicalized to the utmost. It is not our society which is made foreign, but the whole Earth, its history and geography, the most common and ordinary things. One is quite surprised to learn that human beings also practise "Elmooarno" (make love) and at the end of their lives undergo "Rascooarno" (die).

'Thus the book is presented in the form of a comic ethnology – which takes the wind out of many sails. Just as ethnologists enjoy larding their writings with words borrowed from the peoples they study, so Gurdjieff manages to thoroughly "exoticize" us, so that our lives and our most everyday activities display their underlying structure. Life could be different: things are not simply "as they are".

'And of course other fields are involved, as well as ethnology. Through this infinitely simple and infinitely effective process, Gurdjieff perfidiously incites us to ask questions: first, of course, to question the authority of science. But also – and even more disconcerting – to question the very reality of its findings. Everything is affected – physics, chemistry, biology. For it goes without saying that Gurdjieff is not satisfied only to substitute words of his own devising for those we use in everyday life. Generalizing the process, he replaces our entire science with another, and our "laws of nature" – as we call them – with a whole other system, described, of course, in a pompous, rebarbative language. Never mind the value of this system for the moment. The important thing here is once again the disorienting and "diabolic" effect, for in "explaining" all phenomena by laws unknown to Earth science, Gurdjieff insinuates a fundamental doubt. Is Einstein right? But what is there in Einstein which is not in the law of Triamazikamno or of Heptaparaparshinokh? Perhaps we do obtain some results, but not because we know the laws, rather because we have glimpsed certain aspects of much more general laws which we do not know. To tell the truth, here one tends to forget that the *Tales* are, after all, a work of fiction. Thoroughly bewildered, we are ready to admit that the sun gives neither heat nor light, that the moon is a nascent planet, not a dead one, and so on. Without realizing it we reach the point of *taking Gurdjieff at his word*, so that we have to make a certain effort to *wake up*, to understand the game we have just been taken in by, and also to see that in life we are perhaps taken in by just such a game.

'I hasten to add that Gurdjieff's "laws" are definitely not as fantastic as one might think, and that his cosmology may be less absurd than it seems. For the moment, though, this is not what matters: the important thing is to see the process through which Gurdjieff, so to speak, disabuses his reader, forces him to question what he never questions and – last but not least – makes him grasp at first hand what it is that produces that dismal mechanization of thought which lies at the root of so many of our troubles.'[5]

5 Gurdjieff and 'word prostitution'

Gurdjieff went at some length into his literary project, and into the means chosen to implement it, in the first chapter of *Beelzebub's Tales* and the introduction to *Meetings With Remarkable Men*.

First, he writes because he is compelled to do so. No one cared less for 'fame' than Gurdjieff, and for some time his writings were available only to the members of the groups he guided. He insists that his work is not essentially 'literary' in the usual sense of the word. Writing is above all a religious act, as the first paragraph of the *Tales* makes eminently clear;

> Among other convictions formed in my common presence during my responsible, peculiarly composed life, there is one such also – an indubitable conviction – that always and everywhere on the earth, among people of every degree of development of understanding and of every form of manifestation of the factors which engender in their individuality all kinds of ideals, there is acquired the tendency, when beginning anything new, unfailingly to pronounce aloud or, if not aloud, at least mentally, that definite utterance understandable to every even quite illiterate person, which in different epochs has been formulated variously and in our day is formulated in the following words: 'In the name of the Father and of the Son and in the name of the Holy Ghost. Amen.'
> That is why I now, also, setting forth on this venture quite new for me, namely, authorship, begin by pronouncing this utterance and moreover pronounce it not only aloud, but even very distinctly and with a full, as the ancient Toulousites defined it, 'wholly-manifested-intonation.'[1]

Gurdjieff's intention is nothing less than to reach the reader in his deepest being, and in all the regions of his being, mental, emotional and corporeal. In this respect Gurdjieff's books stand utterly distinct from the works of someone like Ouspensky, remarkable as they are, whose scope is necessarily reduced by their overly intellectual character.

Gurdjieff has been much talked about but very little read, and when read, rarely appreciated. The fact is that he is an anomaly. His work cannot be compared with anything else written in this century, nor classified in any precise genre. Hence the disaffection of those head-hunters of the mind, the critics: finding themselves unable to reduce what is so vast that they cannot even grasp it, they ignore or despise it – this is proved, I think, by those critical commonplaces to the effect that Balzac wrote badly, and Victor Hugo was stupid. Nowadays one hears that Gurdjieff was dangerous, dishonest. People steered clear of him, and after his death they steer clear of his work, which is simultaneously fiction, epic poem, satire and auto-biography – as well as constituting a world-view unknown to those who claim that thinking is their calling. The perfection of Gurdjieff's work has seldom been recognized.

Yet as far back as 1956 a writer like Manuel Rainoird was praising 'his literary mastery, so clearly displayed (the genres he calls into play leave our elegant efforts far behind)'.[2] Rainoird adds:

> I feel the strong necessity, once having read *Beelzebub's Tales to His Grandson: An Objectively Impartial Criticism of the Life of Man* – if I say 'read' it is for want of a better word, for the work is much more than that suggests, like an infinitely testing trial, a substance both assimilable and unassimilable by every organ – to pronounce in the midst of my stunned astonishment the words 'great' and 'new'. But as I also run my eye through the library of contemporary fiction, I realize that here there is no possible term of comparison, and that when it comes to 'great' and 'new' there is no book to approach it – what work of philosophy, science, legend or history? And yet it is our history which is in question, yours and mine, universal and personal.[3]

The greatness lies in the undertaking, the total novelty in the *tone*, that particular tone (as Rimbaud's dawns are 'particular') which makes a major work, and which has never been heard or conveyed by those whom Gurdjieff calls 'ordinary patented-writers'.

The *Tales* begin with a reiterated profession of faith:

> In any case I again repeat – in order that you should well
> remember it, but not as you are in the habit of remembering other
> things and on the basis of which are accustomed to keeping your
> word of honor to others or to yourself – that no matter what
> language I shall use, always and in everything, I shall avoid what
> I have called the 'bon ton literary language.'[4]

'Bon ton' was undoubtedly what he ridiculed the most; and education, as we understand it, was what he saw as the most grievous
problem of all. Literature seemed to him to be one of the noblest of
disciplines, sorrily reduced in this century to what he harshly describes as 'the development of "word prostitution".'[5] Read the introduction to *Meetings With Remarkable Men*, with its merciless speech by
the elderly cultured Persian. Anyone who has prided himself on his
skill with the pen, and anybody who dips complacently into the
stagnant water of contemporary prose and cadences – when these
amount to nothing more than futile yet injurious linguistic manipu-
lations – if there is a jot of honesty left in him, will not be able to
read that speech without being overwhelmed by the power of those
basic truths which are the common province of the masters, and which
in their apparent triteness we tend to bypass, to our own detriment,
when instead we should pay them the closest attention.

The journalism whose faults are condemned by the genius of
Balzac in *Illusions perdues* rots language and rots thought. With trivial
games on the one hand, and continual lying on the other, the spirit
becomes irretrievably corrupted:

> 'According to my conviction, which has finally become as firm as
> a rock – and anyone thinking more or less impartially will come to
> the same conclusion – it is chiefly owing to this journalistic
> literature that any man who tries to develop by the means avail-
> able in contemporary civilization acquires a thinking faculty
> adequate, at the very most, for "the first invention of Edison",
> and in respect of emotionality develops in himself, as Mullah
> Nassr Eddin would say, "the fineness of feeling of a cow".'[6]

Consequently, one can only turn to those ancient methods some of
which Charles Duits elicits in the essay quoted above, if one wishes
not only to communicate essential information to the reader but also

to act, as Gurdjieff sets out to act, on the reader's entire being.

The dramatic question which today faces the writer who cares about truth, namely how can sublime words still be uttered without being misunderstood, Gurdjieff settles in an exemplary manner. Just as the sacred *wonder* of the heroes of tragedy metamorphoses into the mere raising of a blasé eyebrow, so, day after day, the holy words love, hope and freedom are watered down; these words, among others, have been tainted and weakened every time they have fallen from the mouths of fanatics and tyrants. How is the original strength of these words to be restored? Gurdjieff either translates them into the language of Karatas or else uses the same unchanging method to clarify their meaning: when he means the vague idea he will say 'love', in inverted commas, and when he means the idea in its fullest sense he will say 'sacred being-impulse of genuine Love'. And this insistence on repeating the words of Karatas, and on solemnly defining ideas, is to my mind one of the strengths of his language, even though it has often been felt as unnecessary emphasis.

What should the reader of the *Tales* guard against, above all? To find that out, all it takes is to read through the familiar expressions which are put between inverted commas in the first pages of the book: the fatal ability to put off anything we wish to do 'till tomorrow', all the 'wealth' people have, the 'professional writers', and their 'instructive-articles', 'patented-writers', 'bon ton literary language' and so on. But the inverted commas may also highlight some just expression used by Beelzebub and his kind: 'active being-mentation', for example, or 'higher being-bodies' or 'being-Partkdolg-duty'.

Thus there is nothing fortuitous in Gurdjieff's style. The *Tales* are a book of initiation, with numerous facets. Again I am obliged to turn to a writer who will illuminate certain aspects of the diverse body of Gurdjieff's work better than I can:

So here is a book which cannot be read as we read our books – which simultaneously attracts and repels us. A book of a stature and inspiration which, although it entirely contains us, bag and baggage, is manifestly far above our heads! It is as if, caught up in that inspiration, engulfed in it and exhorted along the way to behave as something other than children, we were being urged to want what is wanted without our participation. It is like the implacable guard who chivvies and rouses the passengers before the train reaches some frontier, out of sheer kind-heartedness (since he is not involved), so that they will be ready and things will go smoothly.

Here man is seen from above, as he had never previously been seen. This vision from a very great distance – Beelzebub the narrator is the inhabitant of worlds like our own, only far removed, and as an envoy from above he has sometimes had occasion to make flights to the planet Earth – this overview on the scale of our Great Universe engulfs any reader and bathes him in an extraordinarily clear light, so that far from blurring the details, the hidden springs of the human mechanism, it has the effect of revealing them all the more. The more the view embraces, the better it explains by analogy the function and meaning of the creature made in the image of God. Here, distance has a twofold and quite astonishing effect. The greater the height to which Beelzebub goes, the more the confusion of our usual jumble of ideas is dispelled. What emerges is the opposite – we see in high relief what was previously screened and misunderstood. The high has illuminated the low. Infinite spaces have ceased to frighten us. They no longer appear in the void of a bleak futility, produced by the musings of the top mathematician in the open examinations; instead, now that they are peopled – revealing themselves in their tangible aspect as emanations of the affliction of Our deeply-Loving and infinitely patient eternal Creator – they become living, transmitting matter, creative of a new language, matter of which Beelzebub is a more and more conscious emanation, through his merits and his efforts.

Now in spite of this grandeur Beelzebub still remains a kind of standard or model, all other things being equal. His personality is attractive. Deprived of his horns, Beelzebub, devil though he is, has not been exempt from the process of expiation. This was his exile in the solar system Ors, to which our own planet belongs – exile for errors made in his youth, and which greatly resemble our familiar *sins*, with the corollary they imply, the forgetting of man's cosmic functions in the universe, and the concomitant unhappy effects which are impartially noted by Beelzebub, who would like to see them rooted out from inside the three-centred beings of the planet Earth.

What do we know of the meaning of our life on Earth? If G. I. Gurdjieff works within a literary form so that this question may some day occur to us, under certain conditions, he does it like no one else. All commentaries past, present and future, even *In Search of the Miraculous*, are mere pools compared with his ocean. If Gurdjieff tackles his task in one manner only, he has available an arsenal of ways to arouse our interest. Although it is impossible to follow the usual practice of giving a glimpse of what is named or described, it would be an act of charity at least to point out to the dear public, fond of philosophico-literary tracts, that we are actually dealing here with the disconcerting question: 'Who are we, where are we going?', but strongly flavoured, according to a recipe it will not find familiar, with an accompaniment of cymbals and the use of other sonorous and percussive instruments. In this recipe, iced water and itching powder are also involved.

But let me repeat that the reader is not simply *defeated*. He is reading the kind of *roman-fleuve* which, in the long run, will sweep him along with it. The work of demolishing received ideas is not undertaken with the aim of imposing a knowledge which we have not drawn in through our own roots, or which, taken literally, and without genuine links with the inner world, would tend to generate grave misapprehensions. With our minds under such fiendish attack, we give way to the following mental gymnastics: we defend ourselves, we surrender. And if we surrender it is because somewhere around the plexus a warmth may develop – like the air filling in our lungs – by virtue of the representations which have been aroused, as if all at once there had been correspondences established between the superb obscurities of this book and unknown areas of ourselves. In simpler terms, let us recall that certain writings, such as the Song of Solomon, or the Gospel According to St John, were designed to rouse our emotions. The *Tales* are of this nature. There is nothing in them for rigid minds.[7]

This uncommonly accurate account comes from the article quoted at the beginning of this chapter, by the writer Manuel Rainoird.

As that other spiritual master, Georges Saint-Bonnet, would have said, a plague on all 'verbal felicities'. Writing only has meaning when it describes genuine – 'being', as Gurdjieff would say – experience, and the writer is the repository of a teaching worthy of the name. 'The favourite error of present-day literature is emphasis,' said Borges. 'Definitive words, words postulating the wisdoms of soothsayers or angels, or the resolves of a more than human firmness – "unique, never, always, altogether, perfection, complete" – are common currency with *every* writer. They do not think that saying a thing too much is just as clumsy a thing for a writer to do as not saying it at all, that generalization and intensification due to negligence are signs of poverty, and that the reader feels this. Their thoughtlessness is the cause of a depreciation of language.'[8]

Gurdjieff is formidably well armed against any such depreciation. The methods he develops to counter it may be surprising, but they are particularly effective. I feel that it is by success on such a scale that genius is measured. As for his thinking, its originality, at least in this century, and its remarkable cohesion are proof enough of its importance. Add to this that his speech is a *speech of life*, and that once it is taken really seriously it has the power to break down the solid walls of unawareness and indifference, and you have measure enough of its range, when you consider that ours is essentially a day of error and delusion.

6　The myth of the 'organ Kundabuffer'

There is something ludicrous in the succession of causes which Gurdjieff attributes to the tragic singularity of our destiny. The universe is governed, in Gurdjieff's mythology, by a redundant administration which, making all due allowances, is rather like the administration he might have known in his childhood in Russia.

Angels and archangels share the 'cosmic government' among themselves, and form various commissions whose task is to settle one or another problem of 'management'. They bear titles of excessive and sometimes comic solemnity: 'the Arch-Engineer Archangel Algamatant', whom Beelzebub calls 'His Pantemeasurability'; the 'Chief-Common-Universal-Arch-Chemist-Physicist Angel Looisos'; or 'His All-Quarters-Maintainer the Arch-cherub Helkgematios'. Not that these angels or these archangels are presented in a ridiculous light – far from it. But they occasionally prove 'unforeseeing', as Gurdjieff stresses, and it is one of their 'unforeseeingnesses' which is at the root of our folly.

It all begins with the accidental genesis of the Moon – 'this solar system was then still being formed and was not yet "blended" completely with what is called "The Harmony-of-Reciprocal-Maintenance-of-All-Cosmic-Concentrations"'.[1] A comet known as 'Kondoor' was due to cross the space where our own Earth was already turning, but without doing any damage. However:

> as a result of the erroneous calculations of a certain Sacred
> Individual concerned with the matters of World-creation and
> World-maintenance, the time of the passing of each of these
> concentrations through the point of intersection of the lines of

their paths coincided, and owing to this error the planet Earth and the comet 'Kondoor' collided, and collided so violently that from this shock, as I have already told you, two large fragments were broken off from the planet Earth and flew into space.[2]

As a consequence of 'this general cosmic misfortune' our solar system receives 'a whole commission consisting of Angels and Archangels, specialists in the work of World-creation and World-Maintenance, under the direction of the Most Great Archangel Sakaki'. This commission observes that under the influence of a cosmic law called 'Law-of-Catching-Up', the broken-off fragments of the Earth, instead of causing further disasters, are starting to make elliptical orbits around their planet of origin. But in order to prevent them from eventually escaping this influence, the Most High Commission 'decided to take certain measures to avoid this eventuality'.[3]

It is necessary for the Earth to emit vibrations, known as 'askokin', in order to keep its two satellites strictly dependent. Now only organic life can produce these vibrations, and so it is that life appears on our planet.

All living beings, Gurdjieff tells us, are 'Similitudes-of-the-Whole'. Men are eminently such, and 'had in them in the beginning the same possibilities for perfecting the functions for the acquisition of being-Reason as have all other forms of "Tetartocosmoses"* arising throughout the whole Universe'.[4]

Thus far there are no unfortunate consequences of the original 'error':

> But afterwards, just in the period when [men] also, as it proceeds on other similar planets of our great Universe, were beginning gradually to be spiritualized by what is called 'being instinct,' just then, unfortunately for them, there befell a misfortune which was unforeseen from Above and most grievous for them.[5]

This is how we learn something which is no more flattering to ourselves than to the 'administrators of the Megalocosmos', namely the famous myth of the 'organ Kundabuffer', which is one of the great and terrible creations of the ruthless awakener.

After some time has elapsed, the all too diligent Most High Commission decides to make a return visit to our solar system in

---

* Tetartocosmos: in the scale of living beings, all three-brained beings.

order to complete its rescue work. Fearing that men 'would pre-maturely comprehend the real cause of their arising and existence . . . namely, that by their existence they should maintain the detached fragments of their planet,' and apprehensive that they may revolt against their fate and in order to escape it 'would be unwilling to continue their existence', the Commission decides 'provisionally to implant into the common presences of the three-brained beings there a special organ with a property such that, first, they should perceive reality topsy-turvy and, secondly, that every repeated impression from outside should crystallize in them data which would engender factors for evoking in them sensations of "pleasure" and "enjoyment."'[6]

Gurdjieff goes on:

'And then, in fact, with the help of the Chief-Common-Universal-Arch-Chemist-Physicist Angel Looisos, who was also among the members of this Most High Commission, they caused to grow in the three-brained beings there, in a special way, at the base of their spinal column, at the root of their tail – which they also, at that time, still had, and which part of their common presences furthermore still had its normal exterior expressing the, so to say, "fullness-of-its-inner-significance" – a "something" which assisted the arising of the said properties in them.

'And this "something" they then first called the "organ Kundabuffer."'[7]

Later, when it turned out that all danger had disappeared, the 'organ Kundabuffer' was removed from human beings, but what the Most High Commission did not anticipate was that, 'although this astonishing organ and its properties had been destroyed in them, nevertheless, owing to many causes, the consequences of its proper-ties had begun to be crystallized in their presences.'[8]

The consequence was an abnormal proliferation of that unstable, infirm, protean entity, the 'it', which thinks, which feels and which acts in us, and which usurps the place of the 'I', the unique auto-cratic master. The 'it', mobile and malleable, is incapable of setting itself any but immediate, trivial goals, is oblivious of death, ignorant of the supreme truths, and its thinking obeys what Daumal called the 'chameleon' law. The less conscious men are, the more they tend to multiply, for since they develop only one body, the physical body, in themselves, each person produces only too few of the vibrations necessary to the survival of the detached fragments of their planet. And as their degree of consciousness lessens, so the number of individuals grows and grows.

Many are the consequences of the properties of the disastrous 'organ Kundabuffer' which have crystallized in the minds of men. I shall name only the most obvious: inability to think for oneself; harmful identification with one's own 'passions'; inability to imagine the process of one's own death; absence of a will freely ordering itself towards a given end; misunderstanding of the cosmic laws and the means of altering one's destiny as an ordinary man – the list would be too long to complete.

Added to this there is a 'redoubtable' property which bears the name of 'suggestibility':

'This strange trait of their general psyche, namely, of being satisfied with just what Smith or Brown says, without trying to know more, became rooted in them already long ago, and now they no longer strive at all to know anything cognizable by their own active deliberations alone.

'Concerning all this it must be said that neither the organ Kundabuffer which their ancestors had is to blame, nor its consequences which, owing to a mistake on the part of certain Sacred Individuals, were crystallized in their ancestors and later began to pass by heredity from generation to generation.

'But they themselves were personally to blame for it, and just on account of the abnormal conditions of external ordinary being-existence which they themselves have gradually established and which have gradually formed in their common presence just what has now become their inner "Evil-God," called "Self-Calming." '[9]

This 'god' gives us what Mallarmé called 'the insensibility of sky and stones', and builds its throne in the place where our hearts should be. All that is left for us is the tyrannical body and impoverished mind.

Gurdjieff said: 'Such is the ordinary man – an unconscious slave entirely at the service of all-universal purposes, which are alien to his own personal individuality.'[10]

Gurdjieff spent his life giving us the means of escaping this monstrous fate. Let the reader be the judge, if he can, from what follows in this book.

7 'The Terror-of-the-Situation'

It is scandalous that in our civilization the learned – giving this word its broadest sense – are not also the wise. It is scandalous that all weaknesses are permitted in the realm of 'private life', and that our system of education is so designed that it teaches everything except self-knowledge and self-mastery.

These simple remarks form the basis of a teaching whose critics have delighted in underlining its austerity, not to say its ruthless character and ultimate impracticability, whereas all that needed understanding was its realism.

Observation (which makes up three quarters of human genius, as Balzac said) led Gurdjieff to proclaim that 'men are not men', just machines reacting blindly to outside forces, devoid of conscience and will. They are *determined*, and they lay unlawful claims to a freedom of which they have only a negative conception – for them, freedom essentially amounts to the possibility of transgression. If man is a machine, and as long as he remains a machine, there can be no psychological study made of him, because any study belongs to the realm of 'mechanics'.

We must learn what it is that comprises what men call their 'I', and how it works.

Gurdjieff teaches first of all that in the ordinary man there is no unity, that man is governed in turn by a multiplicity of contradictory 'I's', and that if he says 'I' it is a misuse. He said of these 'I's':

Each of them is caliph for an hour, does what he likes regardless of everything, and, later on, the others have to pay for it. And there is no order among them whatever. Whoever gets the upper hand is master. He whips everyone on all sides and takes heed of nothing. But the next moment another seizes the whip and beats him. And so it goes on all one's life. Imagine a country where everyone can be king for five minutes and do during these five minutes just what he likes with the whole kingdom. That is our life.[1]

And indeed, how many thoughts, how many wishes can we claim as our own in the course of a day? The whole problem of determinism and freedom is posed here. That this should be the *first* of the questions put by Gurdjieff is not the least of the signs which may convince us of the importance of his teaching, the more so because he offers an answer, the kernel of which is given by Ouspensky in his short book, *The Psychology of Man's Possible Evolution.*[2]

But *all* the books by Gurdjieff and Ouspensky, and those written by their disciples or by commentators, whether they are for Gurdjieff or against him, all ask this question with the same urgency.

Gurdjieff's basic idea is as follows:

that man as we know him *is not a completed being*; that nature
develops him only up to a certain point and then leaves him,
either to develop further, *by his own* efforts and devices, or to live
and die such as he was born, or to degenerate and lose capacity for
development.[3]

Evolution, stagnation or degeneration are seen as the three 'possible futures' of man. By virtue of what criteria does a man's destiny coincide with one or another of these 'possibilities?' This is one of the fundamental questions.

In other words, are we free to choose our destiny?

Gurdjieff's answers to this question are at once elementary and profound, as good answers nearly always are.

First, if men do not change it is because they do not really *want* to change. Usually they confuse desire with will, and shirk the perseverance and effort without which no genuine will can be formed within them.

Besides, anyone who wants to change himself must know himself, but the fact is that man generally believes that he possesses qualities or faculties which he does not actually have, and he aspires to the possession of higher ones while falsely laying claim to simpler ones. *Man, in fact, does not know himself.* Does not know that he is only a machine, and does not know that the key to all mysteries lies in self-knowledge.

It is extremely important to accept this point. Gurdjieff was unshakable in his insistence on it. During one of their early meetings Ouspensky asked:

'Are there any conditions for joining your group?' . . .

'There are no conditions of any kind,' said G., 'and there cannot be any. Our starting point is that man does not know himself, that he *is not*' (he emphasized these words), 'that is, he is not what he can and what he should be.'[4]

The mankind to which we belong constitutes what Gurdjieff sometimes called the *Circle of the Confusion of Tongues*, in which man is subject to the law of chance and accident.

The concealment of true knowledge, in other words esotericism, giving this word its cloistral sense, has been made necessary by the triumph of the individuals of this Circle, where we witness an inversion of values, a morbid subjectification of these values.

This subjectification is due to the absence of conscience in men. Now absence of conscience is ignorance, and ignorance is slavery.

At this point in the chapter I must make an important digression. Gurdjieff's doctrine – though I feel that this is a dangerous word, because in common speech it is loaded with dogmatic overtones – has certainly been 'rationally' described in works by Ouspensky and Maurice Nicoll, but it is too often forgotten that it was not in this exhaustive and coherent form that Gurdjieff himself taught it:

G. gave the ideas little by little, as though defending or protecting them from us. When touching on new themes for the first time he gave only general principles, often holding back the most essential. Sometimes he himself pointed out apparent discrepancies in the theories given, which were, in fact, precisely due to these reservations and suppressions. The next time, in approaching the same subject, whenever possible from a different angle, he gave more. The third time he gave still more.[5]

Thus Gurdjieff never gave his ideas – or rather the ideas whose receptacle he was – in a 'rhetorical' form. Furthermore, in the work he has left behind, Gurdjieff does not appear, like Ouspensky, as a philosopher but as a storyteller.

It is through myth and legend, fable and story, apologue and parable, closely associated with autobiographical elements – in other words always in a *living* manner – that he offers his teaching.

Any exposition which may be made of it is hence necessarily too 'doctrinal', and furthermore incomplete. I can transcribe the words on to paper, but not the smile or the laughter, and not the gaze that gave weight to those words.

But that smile, that laughter and that gaze are miraculously restored to us in Gurdjieff's books, as long as we read them with simplicity and forget about our parching thirst for rationality.

You can dissect the human machine, methodically describe it and its functions so as to underline its defects and list its failures, and perhaps finally put it back together. That is how Ouspensky works.

Gurdjieff, as I say, worked differently.

In *Beelzebub's Tales to His Grandson* he uses a myth to contrast the beings that we are with those that we ought to be, embodying the former in a figure called Lentrohamsanin, 'chief culprit in the destruction of all the Very Saintly Labors of Ashiata Shiemash', the latter being the symbol of mankind conscious, active and free.

Lentrohamsanin is, *par excellence*, if that is the word to use, the man of the Circle of the Confusion of Tongues. He is first of all the fruit of the incredible vanity of his parents, and then of his 'tutors' and 'teachers':

'When this later great learned being there reached the age of a responsible being, and although he had indeed a great deal of information or, as it is called there, "knowledge," nevertheless, he had absolutely no Being in regard to this information or knowledge which he had acquired.'[6]

I shall deal with this relation of the 'line' of knowledge to the 'line' of being in a later chapter. At this point let it suffice to display the full 'Terror-of-the-Situation' as Gurdjieff reveals it to us:

'When the said Mama's-and-Papa's darling became a learned being there of new formation, then because . . . there was no Being whatsoever in his presence . . . the ambition arose in him to become a famous learned being not only among the beings of Nievia, but also over the whole of the surface of their planet.'[7]

What primarily rules us is not so much love of truth as ambition. This ambition impels us always to prefer the eccentric to the true. We accord ludicrous importance to what has 'never before' been

seen, heard or said. We delight in anything pretty, racy or unexpected. The beautiful frightens us: it is too 'spiritual' in the
Baudelairean sense of the word – we no longer recognize it. We
hardly know how to say more than 'I like' or 'I don't like', and our
motives for saying either are inconceivably poverty stricken.

We complain about our destiny, our ignorance and our weaknesses, although we will never form any objective image either of
ourselves or of reality. We advance our own dullness as an excuse for
ignoring the divine, not realizing that it is we ourselves who are
responsible for this dullness, and that the more we renounce our
essential privilege of consciousness, the more our dullness grows.

But, on the other hand, we have a peculiarly contradictory
attitude towards reality. The 'taste of novelty' becomes a kind of
formalism in us, yet the truth is that we value this 'novelty' only in
so far as it does not cause us unease. If it coincides with the truth, we
either reject it in terror or abjectly shut our eyes to it.

Breton had himself photographed holding a poster adorned with
an inscription from Picabia: 'In order to love something, you have to
have seen and heard it for a long time, you pack of idiots!' Gurdjieff
would have appreciated that remark, and perhaps even adopted it
himself, or rather he would have attributed it to the 'incomparable'
and 'venerable' Mullah Nassr Eddin.

Our thinking is usually sheeplike, but when vanity takes a hand,
we cannot rest until we do something 'new'. Speaking of the 'learned
beings of new formation', Gurdjieff says:

'Certain of them were formed into responsible beings with that
special "organic-psychic-need" which in their speech might be
formulated thus:

"An-irresistible-thirst-to-be-considered-as-learned-by-beings-
around-them-similar-to-themselves"; and such an "psycho-
organic-need" began to engender in them that strange inherency
about which I have many times spoken and which is called by
them "cunning wiseacring." '[8]

The problem which Lentrohamsanin sets himself is not to come to
the assistance of all sentient beings by means of true science, but

'to invent a theory upon a topic which nobody before him had
ever touched upon; and secondly, to inscribe this "invention" of
his upon such a Kashireitleer as nobody had ever before inscribed
or would ever be able to in the future either.'[9]

'Kashireitleer' is one of those 'non-terrestrial' words with which Gurdjieff embellishes *Beelzebub's Tales*, and which discourage or more usually infuriate the reader. The word simply means 'parchment'.

The 'Kashireitleer' of Lentrohamsanin (in the myth which concerns us) lay at the root of the 'destruction of all the Very Saintly Labors of Ashiata Shiemash', and here I must say a few words about this figure. He first appears in the Introduction to *Beelzebub's Tales*, where Gurdjieff explains why Beelzebub was exiled from the planet Karatas and came to our solar system. The reason is that, while still a youth, Beelzebub 'once saw in the government of the World something which seemed to him "illogical"'. He therefore rose in rebellion against 'HIS ENDLESSNESS', who was 'constrained' to banish him, 'notwithstanding his All-lovingness and All-forgiveness', to the planet Mars.[10] It was during his exile that Beelzebub made several visits to the Earth, and he describes these visits to his grandson.

But at the point where this story begins, Beelzebub is no longer in exile. Thanks to the intercession of Ashiata Shiemash, 'a Messenger from our ENDLESSNESS', Beelzebub has been pardoned: 'Our MAKER CREATOR . . . gave him permission to return to the place of his arising.'[11]

Right from the start of the *Tales*, the role of Ashiata Shiemash is seen as central. He is the mediator between God and the fallen angel. Later on, Beelzebub himself presents him to us as the saviour of mankind, in an age when their degeneration was already preventing men from leading 'an ordinary being-existence'.

One has to know the substance of this redeeming work – the work ruined by the disastrous Lentrohamsanin – in order to understand the function ascribed by Gurdjieff to esotericism and the work of the initiate. What first strikes the reader is that the Very Saintly Ashiata Shiemash never addresses the 'ordinary three-brained beings' *directly*. His is a hidden language, accessible only to accomplished beings. The redeeming labour will belong to a brotherhood of initiates whom Gurdjieff calls 'the brotherhood "Heechtvori"', which signified 'Only-he-will-be-called-and-will-become-the-Son-of-God-who-acquires-in-himself-Conscience'.[12]

8 The 'Very Saintly Labors' of Ashiata Shiemash

'The Terror-of-the-Situation' was already obvious at the moment when Shiemash first appeared on Earth, but it is worse still, as we shall see, in the times when Gurdjieff is writing. When Ashiata Shiemash was incarnated, it had become impossible for the wise man to accomplish any task in this world 'through one or other of those three sacred ways of self-perfecting, foreordained by OUR ENDLESS CREATOR HIMSELF, namely, through the sacred ways based on the being-impulses called "Faith," "Hope," and "Love." '[1]

'The endless depreciation of the true currency which is language' – to borrow a phrase of André Breton's – gives human beings no chance whatsoever of understanding the true meaning of these words, which Gurdjieff is compelled always to put in inverted commas.

Faith, Hope and Love are spoiled words and concepts. For the 'three-centered beings of this planet', belief is reduced to 'crystallizing a false conviction'.[2] Faith is founded entirely on subjective data,

> 'it arises dependent upon some or other factors, which have been formed in their common presences, owing as always to the same consequences of the properties of the organ Kundabuffer, such as those singular properties which have arisen in them and which they call "vanity," "self-love," "pride," "self-conceit," and so on.'[3]

It is the same with Love. Ordinary men are incapable even of defining it. No one has any objective idea of it, and nowadays people no longer feel the 'sensation of the sacred being-impulse of genuine

Love', which is 'impartial and nonegoistic'.[4] In his own inimitable style – long, circuitous sentences whose pomp underlines their irony – Gurdjieff writes:

> 'Here, in these times, if one of those three-brained beings "loves" somebody or other, then he loves him either because the latter always encourages and undeservingly flatters him; or because his nose is much like the nose of that female or male, with whom thanks to the cosmic law of "polarity" or "type" a relation has been established which has not yet been broken; or finally, he loves him only because the latter's uncle is in a big way of business and may one day give him a boost, and so on and so forth.'[5]

Lastly, the fate given to Hope is worse still, if that is possible. What men call Hope, and which no longer has any connection with 'the being-impulse of sacred Hope', gives rise in their minds to the 'strange disease "tomorrow"'.[6] 'Thanks to the disease "tomorrow," the three-brained beings there, particularly the contemporary ones, almost always put off till "later" everything that needs to be done at the moment, being convinced that "later" they will do better and more.'[7] Hope in them is hope of everything, no matter what, no matter when: a vague impulse corresponding with who knows what forever unsated craving.

The elements of this analysis, which appears in Chapter 26 of *Beelzebub's Tales*, constitute what Gurdjieff calls the 'Legominism' of Ashiata Shiemash, a Legomininism which goes under the title of 'the Terror-of-the-Situation'.

This notion of 'Legominism' is a very important one in Gurdjieff. The word designates any initiatory method of passing on a truth, and occurs 'from initiates to initiates of the first kind, that is from really meritorious beings'.[8]

If the Legominism of Ashiata Shiemash appears in *Beelzebub's Tales*, it is because the *Tales* are themselves a Legominism. The 'friendly advice written impromptu by the author on delivering this book . . . to the printer' must be taken very seriously. To borrow the word which Jarry used instead of 'preface', it constitutes the *lintel* of the book:

> 'Read each of my written expositions thrice:
> 'Firstly – at least as you have already become mechanized to read all your contemporary books and newspapers.

'Secondly – as if you were reading aloud to another person.
'And only thirdly – try and fathom the gist of my writings.'[9]

But the 'Legominism' of Ashiata Shiemash does not only contain critical elements. There is also the admirable 'Tablet of Commandments' which is the core of Gurdjieff's teaching:

> Faith of consciousness is freedom
> Faith of feeling is weakness
> Faith of body is stupidity.
> Love of consciousness evokes the same in response
> Love of feeling evokes the opposite
> Love of body depends only on type and polarity.
> Hope of consciousness is strength
> Hope of feeling is slavery
> Hope of body is disease.[10]

Unhappily the Faith, Love and Hope of consciousness have utterly disappeared from the human psyche. At the mythical moment when Ashiata Shiemash appears, the Sacred Ways are impracticable. What is to be done then? How is man to be separated from his fantasies, and what is left intact and pure within him?

Gurdjieff's answer is that there is an impulse deep inside us, so deeply embedded that we do not even perceive its reality, 'which impulse exists under the name of *Objective-Conscience*'.[11]

'In the common presences of men-beings all the data exist for the manifestation of the Divine impulse conscience, but . . . this Divine impulse does not take part in their general consciousness'.[12]

Which means, once again, that we see reality upside-down, that what we presumptuously call our conscious life is basically only a kind of slavery, a continual submission of our own being to chance, and hence to a shameful de-formation of a consciousness which, just when it believes that it is breaking free, is instead becoming estranged. Which means that, for man, any ideology is stifling. It means too that the famous alternative of 'transforming the world' or 'changing life' is only a sham, and that only the man who has begun to listen to the 'inner voice' can claim to act, only the man who has understood that it is from the 'subconsciousness' that good impulses come and that 'the objective impulse of Divine-Love' springs.

But how can the being impulse of 'Objective-Conscience' be manifested? In the myth of the Ashiatian organization, in Chapter

27 of the *Tales*, there is a clear account. There we find the image of a suffering God whose 'sorrow is formed . . . from the struggle constantly proceeding in the Universe between joy and sorrow.'[13] The 'emanations-of-the-sorrow', and therefore man's participation in the divine suffering, enable true consciousness to emerge.

To illuminate this passage we could turn to Spinoza's statement that 'Joy is the transition of man from a lesser to a greater perfection. Sorrow is the transition of man from a greater to a lesser perfection.' I discovered this statement, together with a commentary, in an essay published by René Daumal in the *Nouvelle Revue française* in 1934, under the title of 'The non-dualism of Spinoza, or Philosophical dynamite'.[14]

When you learn that Daumal had met Alexandre de Salzmann, himself a disciple of Gurdjieff, in 1930, and that Gurdjieff's teaching was not without influence on his work, the scope of his commentary and the light it may shed on the myth we are studying are in my view very much enhanced.

Daumal writes:

If these propositions were untrue, the world and the very essence of the spirit would be nothing but a sorry farce (it is often quite hard not to believe as much), and it would be better to blow one's brains out straight away. But these definitions are true, although almost unbelievable. Of course one has to know what this joy is. It is not pleasure. It is almost always born in the midst of sufferings. It is Joy willed absurdly *in spite of* the necessary sorrow, it is the very feeling of Liberty willed absurdly *in spite of* the universal determinism. The soul in fact feels Joy when it *acts*, which is to say when it knows, and sorrow when it *suffers*. It follows that in order to understand this doctrine of Joy one must classify all *pleasures undergone*, which man enjoys without making them, under the heading of *Sorrow*, and all the sufferings he may impose upon himself, or actively accept with a view to knowledge, under the heading of *Joy*. And the greatest Joy, which is 'the intellectual Love of God', is 'the Joy that stems from the third kind of knowledge' – ('By the very fact that I know something, I know what it is to know something') – 'accompanied by the idea of God as cause', which is to say: the Joy of a being creating himself and knowing himself as real. And anyone who meditates upon that for an instant will understand that *this Joy is not funny*.

Certainly Gurdjieff's thought does not seem reconcilable with the use made in this text of the adverb 'absurdly'. And 'the greatest Joy' would be not so much 'the intellectual Love of God' as 'the being-Love of God'. But with these reservations I feel it important to stress the points of similarity. First, that 'joy is not pleasure'; that 'pleasures undergone' belong to the world of Sorrow; and that the true Joy 'is not funny'.

To the order of 'pleasures undergone' there unquestionably belong all the degraded forms of love enumerated by Ashiata Shiemash in his analysis of 'the Terror-of-the-Situation'.

And for evidence that the true Joy is 'not funny' I would only cite what Gurdjieff says of the way proposed by Ashiata Shiemash for the salvation of men, which is the way of 'intentional sufferings'.

'We men,' he says, 'are, and must be . . . only suffering.'[15] Yet not blind suffering but conscious suffering, which as Daumal emphasizes deserves in the final analysis to be classified under the heading of Joy. Suffering which arises out of an inner struggle which alone permits the transition 'from a lesser to a greater perfection'. Let us recall what is, according to Gurdjieff, the alternative of our destiny: either 'to feed the moon' (at best stagnating, at worst regressing), or to become 'immortal within the limits of the solar system'[16] – in other words to rise to a higher degree on the scale of realities.

It is through voluntary suffering that such a progression has been made possible. This is the lesson of Ashiata Shiemash. It is his influence that inculcated the idea that 'in the subconsciousness of people there are crystallized and are always present the data manifested from Above for engendering in them the Divine impulse of genuine conscience'.[17]

In order to help them, Ashiata Shiemash associates himself with the members of a brotherhood 'who were working upon that abnormally proceeding functioning of their psyche which they themselves had constated'. The name of this brotherhood, 'Tchaftantouri', means 'To-be-or-not-to-be-at-all'.[18] Under the influence of Shiemash it changes and becomes the 'brotherhood Heechtvori' whose importance has already been indicated.

'What are called "All-the-rights-possessing" brethren' are all those who succeed in acquiring 'ableness-of-conscious-direction-of-the-functioning-of-his-own-psyche'.[19] But these brethren's obligation does not stop here: they must also initiate 'a hundred other beings' by giving them the '"Required-intensity-of-ableness," to be able to convince and persuade not less than a hundred others also'.

These 'All-the-rights-possessing brothers' are the true initiates, and they alone merit the title of 'priest':

'Those beings were called and are still called by this word priest who by their pious existence and by the merits of their acts performed for the good of those around them, stand out so much from the rank and file of the ordinary three-brained beings there, that whenever these ordinary beings there have occasion to remember them, there arises and proceeds in their presences the process called "gratitude." '[20]

Some of the elders among these 'All-the-rights-possessing brothers' were chosen by Shiemash to become 'Great Initiates'. These were the ones

'who had already sensed [the objective impulse of Divine-Love], consciously by their Reason and unconsciously by the feelings in their subconsciousness, and who had full confidence that by certain self-efforts this Divine being-impulse might become and forever remain an inseparable part of their ordinary conscious-ness.'[21]

Each time a being perfects himself by virtue of his conscious efforts, he takes part in the divine suffering, and to that extent alleviates it; if, on the other hand, he lets himself be ruled by the law of accident, if, instead of acting, he suffers it, his fall is inevitable, and he himself becomes a source of sorrow for God.

'Intentional suffering' allows action, from which Joy proceeds. It results from the struggle within ourselves in which 'desires' and 'nondesires' are opposed.

'Non-suffering', negative or passive pleasure, on the other hand, belong to the realm of Sorrow, as Daumal underlined.

Gurdjieff wrote:

'And so, only he, who consciously assists the process of this inner struggle and consciously assists the "non-desires" to predominate over the desires, behaves just in accordance with the essence of our COMMON FATHER CREATOR HIMSELF; whereas he who with his consciousness assists the contrary, only increases HIS sorrow.'[22]

In the myth, prompted by the 'All-the-rights-possessing brothers' and by the 'Great Initiates', mankind becomes conscious of this necessity, and men strive to crystallize 'Objective-Conscience' in themselves. Hence 'those two chief forms of ordinary being-existence abnormally established there' – namely 'their division into numerous communities' and their re-division, inside these communities, into castes or classes – disappear of their own accord.

This twofold anomaly is caused by egoism, which itself is the expression of the triumph of 'personality' over 'essence'. In short, though I shall develop my analysis of these ideas later on, essence represents the true Self, personality the illusory self which is basically the fruit of education. What we call our conscious life is merely the life of our personality, which is wholly subject to the law of accident.

When the impulses of Faith, Hope and Love are debased, they are the faith, hope and love of the personality: credulity, 'the disease "tomorrow"', subjectivity. In most people the essence, the true Self, is weak. It constitutes what Gurdjieff calls the 'subconsciousness', where 'Objective-Conscience' is abnormally located. Thus in our ordinary life it is our consciousness which is fallacious, our subconsciousness which is sincere. To move the 'impulse of Divine-Love' from the latter to the former realm was the work of the Very Saintly Ashiata Shiemash and the 'brotherhood Heechtvori' in Gurdjieff's myth, developing men's essence, and – in the words of the Introduction to *Beelzebub's Tales* – destroying 'in [his] mentation and feelings . . . the beliefs and views, by centuries rooted in him, about everything existing in the world.'

Egoism, the perversion of Love, and the product as I said of education, has deceit as its corollary:

> 'To teach and to suggest to their children how to be insincere with others and deceitful in everything, has become so ingrained in the beings of the planet Earth of the present time, that it has even become their conception of their duty towards their children; and this kind of conduct towards their children they call by the famous word "education."
>
> 'They "educate" their children never to be able and never to dare to do as the "conscience" present in them instinctively directs, but only that which is prescribed in the manual of "bon ton" usually drawn up there just by various candidates for "Hasnamusses".'[23]

Egoism usurps the place of the 'Unique-All-Autocratic-Ruler' in men's psyche; it prevents the manifestation of the individuality, conscience, will and capacity for doing, which are the attributes of the fully achieved being. Egoism and its epiphenomena, 'quite exclusively-particular being-impulses now existing there under the names of "cunning," "envy," "hate," "hypocrisy," "contempt," "haughtiness," "servility," "slyness," "ambition," "double-facedness," and so on and so forth,'[24] also prevent the inner impulse called 'remorse-of-Conscience' from 'lingering long' in the 'common presences' of the 'three-brained beings'. This impulse is a sure sign of the presence in the 'subconsciousness' of 'Objective-Conscience'.

When, under the effect of the 'Very Saintly Labors of Ashiata Shiemash' men at last come to consider one another as 'manifestations of a UNIQUE COMMON CREATOR' and cease to base their relationships on subjective impulses, but 'pay respect to each other only according to the merits personally attained by means of "being-Partkdolg-duty," that is, by means of personal conscious labors and intentional sufferings,' then 'their separate independent communities and the division of themselves in these communities into various castes or classes' disappear.[25]

The leaders of the community are no longer appointed 'by hereditary right nor by election' but by 'difference of age' and by what is called 'essence-power'.

Under the influence of Ashiata Shiemash a great many of the 'abnormal conditions' of human existence completely disappear. First, no one obeys through compulsion any longer, but the respect and deference shown to others are proportional to their 'objective attainments'. Second, 'the process of reciprocal destruction' comes to an end, together with violence, war and the 'irresistible-urge-for-the-periodic-destruction-of-each-other's-existence'.[26] Lastly, there is a considerable decline in both the death rate and the birth rate.

If the first of these points is easy to understand, the others require comment. According to Gurdjieff (I shall say more about this law of his cosmology below), the object of organic life is to produce the vibrations necessary to the normal transmission of higher planetary energy to the Earth. Consciousness produces these vibrations, but in the absence of consciousness in men they can only be produced by the sheer numbers of men and by their tensions. Thus war is a process by which unconscious mankind involuntarily produces the vibrations necessary for the development of the planet, which is, like all cosmic realities, a living being.

To close this chapter I think it is worthwhile to quote Gurdjieff's description in Chapter 27 of *Beelzebub's Tales* of man as 'reformed' by Ashiata Shiemash, before Lentrohamsanin became guilty of 'the destruction of all the Very Saintly Labors':

> 'All the beings of this planet then began to work in order to have in their consciousness this Divine function of genuine conscience, and for this purpose, as everywhere in the Universe, they transubstantiated in themselves what are called the "being-obligolnian-strivings" which consist of the following five, namely:
>
> 'The first striving: to have in their ordinary being-existence everything satisfying and really necessary for their planetary body.
>
> 'The second striving: to have a constant and unflagging instinctive need for self-perfection in the sense of being.
>
> 'The third: the conscious striving to know ever more and more concerning the laws of World-creation and World-maintenance.
>
> 'The fourth: the striving from the beginning of their existence to pay for their arising and their individuality as quickly as possible, in order afterwards to be free to lighten as much as possible the Sorrow of our COMMON FATHER.
>
> 'And the fifth: the striving always to assist the most rapid perfecting of other beings, both those similar to oneself and those of other forms, up to the degree of the sacred "Martfotai" that is up to the degree of self-individuality.'[27]

These rules are clearly those which we ourselves ought to obey if we were at all 'conscious', if we stopped deceiving ourselves and if we took the teaching of the masters truly seriously.

9 The destruction of the 'Very Saintly Labors'

The true 'I' is the one which Lentrohamsanin always ignored, and always prevented from developing. For he is one of those beings whom Gurdjieff calls 'learned beings of new formation', those 'who "learned-by-rote" as much as possible about every kind of vacuous information, such as old women love to relate about what was presumably said in olden times'.[1]

But it appears that there arose within him, under the effect of 'the crystallization of the consequences of the maleficent organ Kundabuffer', those abnormal impulses 'which exist there under the names of "vanity," "self-love," "swagger," and so forth'. Hence the compulsion he felt 'to inscribe this "invention" of his upon such a Kashireitleer as nobody had ever before inscribed'.[2]

And what else should he hold forth about except freedom, the very freedom which he felt he did not fully enjoy within the Ashiatian organization, since in it he was subject to the authority of those who had imposed themselves as leaders by virtue of their age and of the 'essence-power' which they had developed in themselves by their objective merits.

'This Kashireitleer began thus:

'"Man's greatest happiness consists in not being dependent on any other personality whatsoever, and in being free from the influence of any other person, whoever he may be!"'[3]

Bear in mind that according to the tradition to which Gurdjieff claimed allegiance, men were created for a dual purpose: first, 'to help the Moon', which could not live or perfect itself without the 'food' represented by the 'vibrations' they can emit, and second, 'to help God' by perfecting themselves 'to the required gradation of Objective Reason'.

The fundamental idea is that by freeing himself from his own mechanicalness man does not only gain something for himself, and cease to behave as a simple 'apparatus for transforming cosmic substances', but furthermore is able to participate analogously with divine nature.

Here I must quote from the comments on the *Tales* made by Orage, an English disciple of Gurdjieff, in 1927, which are reported by another disciple, C. S. Nott, in his book, *Teachings of Gurdjieff*. Orage said:

> Lentrohamsanin's critique was that of a good philosopher but a pure rationalist. . . . His view was that if a man was created for service he was therefore a slave. Plausibly and craftily he proposed to repudiate this service and attain to absolute freedom. He considered it possible to attain this without making the effort entailed in conscious labour and voluntary suffering.[4]

In other words Lentrohamsanin has a purely egoistic and negative conception of freedom as being a refusal to fulfil a destiny which he, in his limited and biased vision of reality, judges to be unworthy of man. This is because his emotional centre is asleep, which means that Lentrohamsanin is a sick man who has lost the understanding of the heart. This understanding of the heart, Gurdjieff tells us, is the only one that allows 'Objective Conscience' to manifest itself. What comes from the intellect and the intellect alone, what we call our consciousness, is actually a figment, a lie, an illusion.

As Orage said: 'In each of us Lentrohamsanin tries to undo the work of Ashiata Shiemash – an unconscious force working against a conscious force.'

Instead of confronting the problem of ends, Lentrohamsanin's only concern is with present life; he replaces the question 'why?' with the question 'how?'; in place of objective knowledge, he puts personal considerations and a subjective comprehension of one's destiny. Another of Orage's comments may illuminate this point:

'Ashiata Shiemash says: "There is a method by which we can arrive now at an understanding of what *is*."

'Lentrohamsanin says: "There is a means by which we can accommodate ourselves to what is, without understanding it".'

Accommodating ourselves to what is means, in the language of

Lentrohamsanin, to 'strive for our real freedom and our real happiness':

> 'And we can only obtain real freedom and real happiness if we all act as one, that is to say, all for one and one for all. But for this, we must first destroy all that is old.
> 'And we must do so to make room for the new life we shall ourselves create that will give us real freedom and real happiness.
> 'Down with dependence on others!
> 'We ourselves will be masters of our own circumstances. . . .'[5]

All those who were still weak enough not to have understood the cosmic principles of the dual law of conscious labours and intentional suffering, and in whom, because of the 'crystallized consequences of the organ Kundabuffer', was manifested that 'strange inherence' which bears the name of 'suggestibility' – all of these, when they read the Kashireitleer of Lentrohamsanin, had the impression of a *revelation*.

Gurdjieff provides a maliciously thorough account of the usual processes by which men greet what they call 'a new theory'. First, in spite of ourselves, comes spontaneous 'astonishment' and dumbfoundedness in the face of what it is customary to call 'originality'.

After this comes

> 'that usual maleficent what is called "mutual inflation," which had already long been practiced among the learned beings of new formation and chiefly on account of which no true knowledge which has chanced to reach them ever evolves there as it does everywhere else in the Universe, even merely from the passage of time itself; but, on the contrary, even the knowledge once already attained there is destroyed, and its possessors always become shallower and shallower.'[6]

Disciples then declare themselves, according to the notion 'that if anybody becomes a follower of an already well-known and important being, he thereby seems to be to all other beings almost as well known and important himself.'[7]

Lastly two opposing parties emerge, and in the adversaries there crystallizes 'one of their particular properties called "hate"'.[8] At best these confrontations degenerate into polemics, at worst they set off 'the periodic process of reciprocal destruction'. And it is a notorious truth that it is once again in the name of freedom that men kill one another: the myth of the Destruction of the Very Saintly Labors is an illustration of this appalling truth.

Because of this 'hate', a civil war breaks out, ending with the triumph of 'hordes' of 'learned beings'. As soon as these have taken power they institute 'a special what is called "Republic"', and they 'compelled all the surviving beings to accept the ideas of Lentrohamsanin and immediately destroyed everything'.[9] Then this community 'began, as it also usually happens there, "making war" on the neighboring communities for the purpose of imposing upon them also her new form of state-organization'.[10]

Certainly the 'Ashiatian organization' was an aristocracy, but only those who had acquired 'essence-power' through their 'objective merits' had authority over others. At present, leaders and counsellors are elected 'on the basis of equal rights, without distinction of sex or age, by universal, direct, equal, and open ballot', as Lentrohamsanin demanded,[11] but this apparent justice is a sham, for the fact is that in order for 'citizens' to make a rational choice they would have to be impartial. Yet their entire behaviour shows otherwise. Furthermore we have seen how leaders obey the abominable slogan: 'No freedom for the enemies of freedom.' When one knows what a narrow, deluded concept men have of the very idea of freedom, their impatience for it to triumph can only be seen as ridiculous: this 'new form of state-organization' clearly cannot rest until it has subdued the whole world, and given it the incomparable taste of Lentrohamsaninian freedom.

So 'the process of reciprocal destruction' goes on for several centuries, although a certain number of beings 'still continued to conform in their ordinary existence to many of the unprecedentedly wisely foreseen usages of the Very Saintly Ashiata Shiemash for their ordinary being-existence, which usages had already been inseparably fused into their automatically flowing process of daily existence'.[12]

Other circumstances no less grievous than those which brought about the disintegration of the 'Ashiatian organization' further aggravated the Terror-of-the-Situation. Gurdjieff situates the legendary events which presided over the final destruction of the Very Saintly Labors long after the fatal advent of Lentrohamsanin.

At that moment Babylon was ruled by 'a most peculiar Persian king'. The three-brained beings had already developed 'a particular "inherency" thanks to which that being-sensation which is called "happiness-for-one's-being" . . . appears in the presences of your favorites exclusively only when they acquire for their own possession a great deal of that popular metal there called "gold." '[13]

The greed for gold, and the 'maleficent fantastic' belief that it was possible to convert any of the base metals into gold providing one possessed a certain secret, first of all led the Persian king to comb his realm for a 'learned being' who knew it. Since no one did know it, the king decided to organize 'military excursions' in order to get hold of all the learned beings in other communities. After many a campaign he congregated in Babylon all the 'learned beings' he had managed to capture.

'When a little later a fresh craze arose in the presence of this peculiar Persian king, the craze for the process itself of the destruction of the existence of other beings similar to himself, and which supplanted the former craze, he forgot about the learned beings and they began to exist there freely in the city of Babylon awaiting his further directions.'[14]

'Learned beings' with time on their hands do not rest until they find some 'question' to debate. Not that this is a true 'being-necessity', it is just that they have to feed the consuming fire of conferences and meetings which they organize to confront each other. This question, 'the-burning-question-of-the-day', Gurdjieff says, was the following: 'Both the "sorry-learned" and also the ordinary beings of the city of Babylon were very anxious to know whether they had a "soul." '[15]

Various 'catchy theories' vied with each other, but all of them, without exception, were based upon 'two quite opposite assumptions':

'One of these was called the "atheistic" and the other the "idealistic" or "dualistic."

'All the dualistic theories maintained the existence of the soul, and of course its "immortality," and every possible kind of "perturbation" to it after the death of the being "man."

'And all the atheistic theories maintained just the opposite.'[16]

On the occasion of this 'general-planetary-conference',

'the great grandson of Lentrohamsanin . . . who had also become a learned being [presented] an exact copy of the mentioned Kashireitleer, but made on papyrus, the original of which had been inscribed by his great-grandfather . . . whereupon, it occurred – as it had also become proper to the "sorry-learned-beings" of this planet, thanks to their strange Reason – that from one question which interested them, they at once passed to quite another, namely, from the question "of-the-soul" to the question of what is called "politics." '[17]

Once again, the processes already described pursue their course:

'For several months they discussed and argued, and as a result, they this time "split" into parties; that is to say all the learned beings then in the city of Babylon split into two independent what are called "sections," under the following names:
  'The first: "Section of Neomothists."
  'The second: "Section of Paleomothists." '[18]

And once again 'hate' crystallizes, and 'civil war' nearly breaks out. But we have seen that the master of Babylon was that 'peculiar Persian king', who was nothing less than a tyrant.

'A number of these learned beings were executed by him, others were imprisoned with lice, and still others were dispatched to places, where even now, as Mullah Nassr Eddin would say, "French champagne" could not be taken.'[19]

Nevertheless, some of these 'learned beings' escape the massacre, and these 'continued by momentum their wiseacring the basis of which they made – of course, not consciously but simply mechanically – those two leading questions which had arisen and which had been the "questions-of-the-day" during the said Babylonian events'.[20]

'Hate' crystallizes in their psyche yet again, and 'the processes of mass reciprocal-destruction' ensue. But some beneficial customs do survive here and there, until the day 'when "hordes" of Europeans with the arch-vainglorious Greek called "Alexander-of-Macedonia" at their head'[21] join in the battle and, by laying waste Asia, bring about the annihilation of whatever traces of the Ashiatian laws may still have survived there.

10   'Fruits of former civilizations'

The accursed legacy of Lentrohamsanin was reaped by 'those two powerful communities there named "Greeks" and Romans."' These communities had become powerful in the terrestrial sense of the word because they had developed 'more means for the processes of reciprocal destruction' than any others. When they had secured their hegemony they turned out to be just as bad for the human race as Lentrohamsanin had been, aggravating the Terror-of-the-Situation still further, if that were possible:

> 'Not only did they then, as I have already said, make a clean
> sweep from the face of that unfortunate planet of the last results
> beneficial for all the three-brained beings of all subsequent
> epochs, and even of all traces of the memory of the Very Saintly
> Labors of the Essence-loving Ashiata Shiemash, but they were
> also the cause that real "nonsense" already proceeds in the
> Reasons of the contemporary favorites of yours, and that there is
> completely atrophied in them that "fundamental-being-impulse"
> which is the main lever of objective morality, and which is called
> "organic shame."'[1]

Faulty use of the intellect and bad or perverse use of sex – these are essentially 'the fruits of former civilizations and the blossoms of the contemporary' ('former' means prior to our own wretched point of view).

Ignorance, vanity and the now deeply entrenched habit of 'wiseacring' means that not only are men ignorant of their nature as 'three-brained beings' but also they allow their centres one by one to waste away and die.

Death, in fact, is not what people believe it to be – it is not a tragic and sublime moment when the planetary body is stilled for ever. Death is even more ignominious: it is *progressive*. 'Many people die long before their physical death.'[2]

'It happens fairly often that essence dies in a man while his personality and his body are still alive. A considerable percentage of the people we meet in the streets of a great town are people who are empty inside, that is, they are actually *already dead*.'[3]

Mind and heart stop *living* inside them. Feelings and ideas have become a matter of sheer chance, and are no longer anything but blind forces acting accidentally, although in a sense necessarily, because they are under sway of circumstances.

Such is the outcome of a system of education which has never allowed us either to think for ourselves or to feel or love freely.

The chapter in which Gurdjieff describes the accursed triumph of Greco-Roman civilization is so powerful and so explosive, its content is so contrary to all the customary analyses, that it is almost impossible to convey its particular flavour in a summary. I can only provide an extract of some length, in the hope that it may be *heard* as Hassein heard it, both with wonder and sadness.

'And so, my dear boy, the beings of these two groups were one of the chief causes that the Reasons of the contemporary favorites of yours have become mechanical, and that the data for engendering the impulse of being-shame have become completely atrophied in them.

'The Greeks were the cause why the Reasons of the three-brained beings there began gradually to degenerate and ultimately became so degenerate that among contemporary beings it is already as our dear Mullah Nassr Eddin says, "a-real-mill-for-nonsense."

'And the Romans were the cause why as a result of successive changes, those factors are never crystallized in the presences of the contemporary three-brained beings there, which in other three-brained beings engender the impulse called "instinctive shame"; that is to say, the being impulse that maintains what are called "morals" and "objective morality."

'Thus it was that those two communities arose there, which afterwards, as it often happens there, became very solid and powerful for a definite period. And the history of their further maleficent "prepared inheritance" for the beings of subsequent generations is as follows:

'According to the investigations of our mentioned countryman, it seems that the earliest ancestors of the beings of the community, which was later called "Greece," were often obliged, on account of the frequent storms at sea which hindered them in their marine occupations , to seek refuge during the rains and winds, in sheltered places, where out of boredom, they played various "games" which they invented for their distraction.

'As it later became clear, these ancient fishermen amused themselves at first with such games as children now play there – but children, it must be remarked, who have not yet started contemporary schooling – because the children there who do go to school have so much homework to do, consisting chiefly of learning by rote the "poetry" which various candidate Hasnamusses have composed there, that the poor children never have time to play any games.

'Briefly, these poor bored fishermen played at first the ordinary children's games already established there long before; but afterwards when one of them invented a new game called "pouring-from-the-empty-into-the-void," they were all so pleased with it that thereafter they amused themselves with that alone.

'This game consisted in formulating some question always about some "fiddle-faddle" or other, that is to say, a question about some deliberate piece of absurdity, and the one to whom the question was addressed had to give as plausible an answer as possible.

'Well, it was just this same game that became the cause of all that happened later.

'It turned out that among those ancient bored fishermen, there were several so "bright" and "ingenious" that they became expert in inventing, according to the principle of the peculiar "game," very long explanations.

'And when one of them discovered how to make what was afterwards called "parchment" from the skin of the fish called "shark," then some of these skillful fellows, just to "swagger" before their companions, even began inscribing these long explanations of theirs on these fishskins, employing those conventional signs which had been invented earlier, for another game called "mousetrap."

'Still a little later, when these bored fishermen had already given place to their descendants, both these inscribed fishskins and the craze for the said peculiar "game" passed on to the latter by inheritance; and these various new inventions, both their own and their ancestors', they called first by the very high-sounding name "science."

'And from then on, as the craze for "cooking up" these sciences passed from generation to generation, the beings of that group, whose ancestors had been simple Asiatic fishermen, became "specialists" in inventing all kinds of sciences as these.

'These sciences, moreover, also passed from generation to generation and a number of them have reached the contemporary beings of that planet almost unchanged.

'And hence it is that almost a half of what are called the "egoplastikoori" arising in the Reason of the contemporary beings of that ill-fated planet, from which what is called a "being-world-outlook" is in general formed in beings, are crystallized just from the "truths" invented there by those bored fishermen and their subsequent generations.

'Concerning the ancient shepherds who later formed the great powerful community called "Rome," their ancestors also were often forced, on account of bad weather, to put their flocks into sheltered places, and to pass the time together somehow or other.

'Being together, they had "various talks." But when everything had been talked out and they felt bored, then one of them suggested that as a relief they should take up the pastime which they called for the first time "cinque-contra-uno" (five-against-one), an occupation which has been preserved down to the present time, under the same name, among their descendants who continue to arise and exist there.

'So long as only the beings of the male sex then engaged in that occupation, everything went "quietly and peacefully," but when a little later their "passive halves," that is to say their women, also joined in, who, immediately appreciating it, soon became addicted to it, they then gradually attained in these "occupations" such "finesses," that even if our All-universal Arch-cunning Lucifer should rack his honorable brains, he could not even invent a tithe of the "turns" these erstwhile shepherds then invented and "prepared" for the beings of the succeeding generations of that ill-fated planet.

'And so, my boy, when both these independent groupings of terrestrial three-brained beings multiplied and began acquiring every variety of those effective "means," namely, the means of reciprocal destruction, whose acquisition is the usual aim of all communities there during all periods of their existence, they then began carrying out these "processes" with other independent communities there – for the most part, of course, with the less powerful communities, and occasionally among themselves.

'Here it is extremely interesting to notice that when periods of peace occurred between these two communities there – communities of almost equal strength in respect of the possession of efficient means for the processes of reciprocal-destruction – the beings of both groups whose places of existence were adjacent often came into contact and had friendly relations with each other, with the result that little by little they picked up from each other those specialties which had first been invented by their ancestors and which had become proper to them. In other words, the result of the frequent contact of the beings of those two communities was that the Greek beings, borrowing from the Roman beings all the finesses of sexual "turns," began arranging their what are called "Athenian nights," while the Roman beings, having learned from the Greek beings how to cook up "sciences," composed their later very famous what is called "Roman law."

'A great deal of time has passed since then. The inventors of both those kinds of being-manifestation have already long been destroyed, and their descendants who chanced to become "powerful" have been destroyed also. And now . . . the contemporary three-brained beings of that planet spend, even with emotion, more than half their existence and being-energy, acquired somehow or other in absorbing and actualizing unconsciously and sometimes even consciously those two ideals, the initiators of whose arising were the said bored Asiatic fishermen and shepherds.

'Well then, my boy, later on, it seems, when both these groupings of your favorites acquired many of the said efficient means for the successful destruction of the existence of beings like themselves, and when they had become quite expert in persuading, or by potency of their means compelling beings of other countries to exchange their inner convictions for those ideals invented by their ancestors, then, as I have said, they first conquered the neighboring communities situated on the continent Europe, and afterwards, for the same purpose, with the help of the hordes they collected during that period, turned towards the continent Asia.

'And there already on the continent Asia, they began spreading that maleficent influence of theirs, first among beings populating the western shores of that continent – in whom, as I have already said, being-impulses for a more or less normal being-existence had been implanted during centuries – and afterwards, they gradually began advancing into the interior.

'This advance of theirs into the interior of the continent Asia proceeded very successfully, and their ranks were constantly being increased, chiefly because the learned beings who had been in Babylon then continued everywhere on the continent Asia to infect the Reasons of beings with their Hasnamussian political ideas.

'And they were also helped very much by the fact that there were still preserved in the instincts of the Asiatic beings the results of the influences of the initiates and priests, disciples of the Very Saintly Ashiata Shiemash, who in their preachings had inculcated among other things, one of the chief commandments of Ashiata Shiemash which declared:

' "Do not kill another even when your own life is in danger."

'Profiting by all this, these former fishermen and shepherds were very easily able to advance, destroying on the way all those who declined to worship the "gods" they themselves had finally acquired, that is to say, their fantastic "science" and their phenomenal depravity.

'At first these "sowers-of-evil" for all the three-brained beings there of all the succeeding generations, arising on the continent Europe, and especially the Greeks, moving into the interior of the continent Asia, acted if slowly nevertheless effectively.

'But when some time later there appeared and stood at the head of what is called an "army" that completely formed Arch-Vainglorious Greek, the future Hasnamuss, Alexander of Macedonia, then from that time on, there began to proceed that clean sweep of the last remnants of the results of the very saintly intentional labors of our now Common Cosmic Most Very Saintly Ashiata Shiemash, and again there was resumed, as it is said, the "old-old-story." [4]

That 'old-old-story' is still being told to this day, with further episodes as pernicious as the old ones, the result being that our life is nothing but a huge joke. To unlearn the catchwords and clichés inculcated in us by those who claimed to be our teachers is one of the first imperatives if we want to develop anything more than the ghost of an 'I' in ourselves.

Under the influence of Lentrohamsanin and his descendants, in place of the 'being-obligolnian-strivings'[5] men develop seven other tendencies constituting what the *Tales* call the 'Naloo-osnian-spectrum-of-impulses'.

'If these . . . are described according to the notions of your favorites and expressed in their language, they might then be defined as follows:

(1) Every kind of depravity, conscious as well as unconscious

(2) The feeling of self-satisfaction from leading others astray

(3) The irresistible inclination to destroy the existence of other breathing creatures

(4) The urge to become free from the necessity of actualizing the being-efforts demanded by Nature

(5) The attempt by every kind of artificiality to conceal from others what in their opinion are one's physical defects

(6) The calm self-contentment in the use of what is not personally deserved

(7) The striving to be not what one is.'[6]

These impulses single out those human beings who in their life-times merit the title of 'candidate Hasnamussian'. After their death, and according to the gravity of their sins, they become 'Hasnamuss-individuals', or even 'Eternal-Hasnamuss-individuals', and while the latter inhabit the planet 'Retribution', the former, who still have the chance of redeeming themselves, are allotted to three small planets existing under the names of 'Remorse-of-Conscience', 'Repentance' and 'Self-Reproach'.[7]

11 The four 'bodies' of man

If Ashiata Shiemash is the symbol of a complete man, of the initiate, the 'elect', Lentrohamsanin is on the contrary a pitiless portrait of ourselves, our ignorance and our presumption.

As we have seen, this 'later great learned being' allows himself to be ruled exclusively by self-love and by ambition. His own blindness and thirst for fame lead him to preach a 'liberation' which is nothing but total slavery. His first crime is in fact the rejection of the master, because he is incapable of discerning 'objective merits' in him. Not that the fault is altogether his; his parents, in their excessive love of their son, and through him of themselves, may be even more to blame. Accustomed as he is to praise, and even to adulation, he is so convinced of his own greatness that not only can he not bring himself to submit, but he cannot rest until he has caused a stir by producing some new theory.

The whole trouble stems from the want of proportion in Lentrohamsanin between knowledge and being, essence and personality.

According to Gurdjieff, while we accept that there are degrees of knowledge, we do not know that the same is true of being, and that '*knowledge* depends on *being*'.[1] 'Being' for us means 'existence', but it is possible to exist in different ways and on different levels. There is already a great difference between the being of a stone and the being of a tree, and again between the being of a tree and the being of a man. But we hold the false belief that there are no degrees within human existence. Whereas Gurdjieff says that there may be just as much distance between one man and another as between stone and tree, tree and man.

Lentrohamsanin is the type of the 'intellectual' only one of whose 'centres' is normally developed. He is the man of reason, who lacks Objective-Conscience, the man of discourse, who lacks Knowledge and Faith. He exists, but he *is* not. He may *know*, but he has no power to *do*.

In such a man, '*Everything happens*.'[2] In such a man, 'it' loves or does not love, 'it' wants, 'it' thinks, 'it' rebels, 'it' judges. But there is no true 'I' except as a word. He *knows*, but he does not *understand*. For understanding requires being and knowledge to have developed harmoniously side by side. In Gurdjieff's terminology, which I shall describe further below, Lentrohamsanin is a 'weak yogi', 'a man who knows a great deal but can do nothing, a man who *does not understand* what he knows, a man without *appreciation* . . . for whom there is no difference between one kind of knowledge and another'.[3]

Man has this weakness in this being because he lives in sleep. Working on himself above all means reflecting on the ways of awakening himself, that is, of changing his *being*. Developing his being is developing the man within, who alone can escape from the state of 'mechanicalness':

> 'Exteriorly man's being has many different sides: activity or passivity; truthfulness or a tendency to lie; sincerity or insincerity; courage, cowardice; self-control, profligacy; irritability, egoism, readiness for self-sacrifice, pride, vanity, conceit, industry, laziness, morality, depravity; all these and much more besides make up the being of man.
>
> 'But all this is entirely *mechanical* in man.'[4]

The man within, on the other hand, is a unified man, possessing 'a permanent center of gravity'.[5] This means that, conscious of the absurdity of his fate, of the mechanicalness of his life, he orders his existence to an end which must necessarily be that of freeing himself from external influences: 'To become free, to be liberated from slavery: this is what a man ought to strive for when he becomes even a little conscious of his position.'[6]

As we have seen, man does not know himself. He does not know his own weakness, and fails to recognize his own possibilities. Now Gurdjieff tells us that he has no right to the name of man except when he is conscious – conscious not only of himself but also and above all of the possible evolution of his 'I'. But nothing in everyday life gives him access to this latter form of consciousness. Many have been the voices, even if only among true poets, denouncing the idiotic character of our life, but cut off as they were from the Source, and from a tradition of which Gurdjieff is one of the repositories, once they had grasped the Terror-of-the-Situation what could they do but uselessly rebel or die of despair?

These men were, as we all are, in prison. But their enormous superiority over other men was to know it. And their despair grew out of their being unable to make their escape. 'No one can escape from prison,' said Gurdjieff, 'without the help of those *who have escaped before*. Only they can say in what way escape is possible or can send tools, files, or whatever may be necessary.'[7]

This prison is the Circle of the Confusion of Tongues, the 'exoteric' world in which we are subject to the law of chance and accident. We come into the world in this prison, of which our education builds the walls higher and casts the bars thicker. Only an *esoteric* teaching can enable a man to escape, but in general man does not know or refuses to admit that he is in prison – in fact this is one of the reasons why the teaching of the masters is described as *esoteric*.

'Why is this knowledge 'so carefully concealed'? asks Ouspensky. 'It is not concealed,' Gurdjieff replies.

'No one is concealing anything; there is no mystery whatever. But the acquisition or transmission of true knowledge demands great labor and great effort both of him who receives and of him who gives. And those who possess this knowledge are doing everything they can to transmit and communicate it to the greatest possible number of people, to facilitate people's approach to it and enable them to prepare themselves to receive the truth. But knowledge cannot be given by force to anyone. . . .'[8]

Man is a slave, but you cannot free *in spite of himself* a man who denies being a slave. To know one's nature as a slave is to have thrown off a good many chains already, to be capable of *moving*.

What is the aim of the teaching?

'It can only show the best way for men to attain whatever aims they may have. The question of aim is a very important question. Until a man has defined his own aim for himself he will not be able even to begin "to do" anything.'[9]

And what other aim can a slave have, to begin with, except to free himself, which means knowing himself, knowing his powers and moving himself by shaking off every fetter. But before knowing and being capable of moving oneself, self-study is necessary.

'Self-study is the work or the way which leads to self-knowledge.

'But in order to study oneself one must first learn *how to study*, where to begin, what methods to use. A man must learn how to study himself, and he must study the methods of self-study.

'The chief method of self-study is self-observation. Without properly applied self-observation a man will never understand the connection and the correlation between the various functions of his machine, will never understand how and why on each separate occasion everything in him "happens." '[10]

Furthermore, even before we come to observe ourselves, in order for this observation to bear fruit we have to know *what we are capable of*. 'Only by understanding the correct sequence of development possible will people cease to ascribe to themselves what, at present, they do not possess, and what, perhaps, they can only acquire after great effort and great labor.'[11]

The tradition which Gurdjieff claimed to follow, 'an ancient teaching, traces of which may be found in many systems, old and new',[12] asserts that if man reaches the final stage of his possible development he is then composed of four bodies.

The first of these bodies, which we all possess, is the 'carnal' or 'physical' body, or the 'planetary' body, as Gurdjieff himself calls it in *Beelzebub's Tales*. The second body is the 'natural' or 'astral' body; the third is the 'spiritual' or 'mental' body; the fourth is the 'divine' or 'causal' body. (Concerning this last adjective, Ouspensky comments: 'That is, the body which bears the *causes* of its actions within itself, is independent of external causes, and is the *body of will*.')[13]

Gurdjieff tells us that the same distinction operates in other teachings in the form of a series of images: the first is the *carriage* (body), the second the *horse* (feelings, desires), the third the *driver* (mind) and the fourth the *master* (I, consciousness, will).

Such as we are, we only possess the first of these four bodies. Not that we do not nurse (the verb is an apt one) desires and thoughts (assuming that we have the slightest doubt that we are endowed with consciousness and will) but that they are, as we shall see, emanations of the lower centres in man: 'The physical body ... has all the functions analogous to those of the higher bodies, though of course they differ from them considerably.'[14]

In the Circle of the Confusion of Tongues, everything is indeed subject to the physical body, and the reality of other bodies is an illusion. The physical body is comparable to an automaton, it represents the 'man-machine' which Gurdjieff bluntly accuses us all of being – subject in all things, no matter what it thinks, to purely external influences. Even art, poetry and thought do not escape the ferocity of his criticism (of course this does not include the case of those who, as creators in one or another of these spheres, were also *masters* in the spiritual sense of the word). But as a general rule, 'Men are machines and nothing but mechanical actions can be expected of machines.'[15]

In the whole man, on the other hand, all functions stem not from the 'physical' but from the 'causal' body.

Individuality, consciousness and will are its essential attributes. And it is the 'causal' body which rules all the others.

1st body	2nd body	3rd body	4th body
Carnal body	Natural body	Spiritual body	Divine body
'Carriage' (body)	'Horse' (feelings, desires)	'Driver' (mind)	'Master' (I, consciousness, will)
Physical body	Astral body	Mental body	Causal body

Figure 11.1

Another image proposed by Gurdjieff and borrowed, as he tells us, from 'an Eastern teaching' is that of 'a vessel or retort'. It is filled with various metallic powders which have no definite connections with each other. With every shake, and every change of the retort's position, these unstable powders shift, and the loose particles move about, now visible on the surface, now disappearing. 'Science calls this state of the powders the state of mechanical mixture', and this is 'an exact picture of our psychic life'.[16]

The only way to 'stabilize' the mixture is to fuse it by lighting a fire under the retort. Once fused, the mixture symbolically represents for us the acquisition of a second body, something indivisible, a genuine 'individuality'. But melting the powders requires fire, which is obtained by a 'friction' which is the struggle within ourselves between 'yes' and 'no', 'nondesires' and 'desires'.

This is still not enough. 'The chemical compound obtained by fusion possesses certain qualities, a certain specific gravity, a certain electrical conductivity, and so on.' We have to work to increase the number of its properties – for example: 'It may be possible to magnetize it, to make it radioactive, and so on.'[17] Hence the third body.

But it would be good to make sure that these new properties are not ephemeral. Once they are fixed and become permanent, the fourth body metaphorically appears.

One of the 'properties' of the whole man who possesses the fourth body is immortality.

'All religions and all ancient teachings contain the idea that, by acquiring the fourth body, man acquires immortality; and they all contain indications of the ways to acquire the fourth body, that is, immortality.'[18]

To return to the image of carriage, horse and driver in their relation to the master, a point that Gurdjieff specially stressed was the importance of *connections*: between master and driver, the voice; between driver and horse, the reins; between horse and carriage, the shafts. It is not enough to possess the four bodies. There must also be communication between the four, in the normal hierarchic order, otherwise the physical body – the carriage – will take over everything again: neither the horse (the feelings), nor the driver (the mind), nor the master (the I) be able to act if the horse is not harnessed, if the driver does not know where the reins are, or if he is sleeping (assuming that he at least speaks the same language as his master). 'There exist four quite different situations,' Gurdjieff says.

'In one case all the functions are controlled by the physical body. It is active; in relation to it everything else is passive. In another case the second body has power over the physical. In the third case the "mental" body has power over the "astral" and the physical. And in the last case the fourth body has power over the first three.'[19]

12 A true likeness of 'man' (extract from *Beelzebub's Tales*)

This is a true likeness of man as Gurdjieff portrays him. Not man as he should or could be, but, on the contrary, as he allows himself to be, ignorant as he is of his own nature and destiny, and slavishly subject to the familiar law of chance and accident:

A man as a whole with all his separately concentrated and functioning localizations, that is to say, his formed and independently educated 'personalities,' is almost exactly comparable to that organization for conveying a passenger, which consists of a carriage, a horse, and a coachman.

It must first of all be remarked that the difference between a real man and a pseudo man, that is between one who has his own 'I' and one who has not, is indicated in the analogy we have taken by the passenger sitting in the carriage. In the first case, that of the real man, the passenger is the owner of the carriage; and in the second case, he is simply the first chance passer-by who, like the fare in a 'hackney carriage,' is continuously being changed.

The body of a man with all its motor reflex manifestations corresponds simply to the carriage itself; all the functionings and manifestations of feeling of a man correspond to the horse harnessed to the carriage and drawing it; the coachman sitting on the box and directing the horse corresponds to that in a man which people call consciousness or mentation; and finally, the passenger seated in the carriage and commanding the coachman is that which is called 'I.'

The fundamental evil among contemporary people is chiefly that, owing to the rooted and widespread abnormal methods of education of the rising generation, this fourth personality which should be present in everybody on reaching responsible age is entirely missing in them; and almost all of them consist only of the three enumerated parts, which parts, moreover, are formed arbitrarily of themselves and anyhow. In other words, almost every contemporary man of responsible age consists of nothing more nor less than simply a 'hackney carriage,' and one moreover, composed as follows: a broken-down carriage 'which has long ago seen its day,' a crock of a horse, and, on the box, a tatterdemalion, half-sleepy, half-drunken coachman whose time designated by Mother Nature for self-perfection passes while he waits on a corner, fantastically daydreaming, for any old chance passenger. The first passenger who happens along hires him and dismisses him just as he pleases, and not only him but also all the parts subordinate to him.

Continuing this analogy between a typical contemporary man, with his thoughts, feelings, and body, and a hackney carriage, horse, and coachman, we can clearly see that in each of the parts composing both organizations there must have been formed and there must exist its own separate needs, habits, tastes, and so on, proper to it alone. From the varied nature of their arising, and the diverse conditions of their formation, and according to their varying possibilities in each of them there must inevitably have been formed, for instance, its own psyche, its own notions, its own subjective supports, its own viewpoints, and so on.

The whole totality of the manifestations of human mentation, with all the inherencies proper to this functioning and with all its specific particularities, corresponds almost exactly in every respect to the essence and manifestations of a typical hired coachman.

Like all hired coachmen in general, he is a type called 'cabby.' He is not entirely illiterate because, owing to the regulations existing in his country for the 'general compulsory teaching of the three R's,' he was obliged in his childhood to put in an occasional attendance at what is called the 'parish church school.'

Although he himself is from the country and has remained as ignorant as his fellow rustics, yet rubbing shoulders, owing to his profession, with people of various positions and education, picking up from them, by bits here and bits there, a variety of expressions embodying various notions, he has now come to regard everything smacking of the country with superiority and contempt, indignantly dismissing it all as 'ignorance.'

In short, this is a type to whom applies perfectly the definition, 'The crows he raced but by peacocks outpaced.'

He considers himself competent even in questions of religion, politics, and sociology; with his equals he likes to argue; those whom he regards as his inferiors, he likes to teach; his superiors he flatters, with them he is servile; before them, as is said, 'he stands cap in hand.'

One of his chief weaknesses is to dangle after the neighboring cooks and housemaids, but, best of all, he likes a good hearty tuck-in, and to gulp down another glass or two, and then, fully satiated, drowsily to daydream.

To gratify these weaknesses of his, he always steals a part of the money given him by his employer to buy fodder for the horse.

Like every 'cabby' he works as is said always 'under the lash,' and if occasionally he does a job without being made, it is only in the hope of receiving tips.

The desire for tips has gradually taught him to be aware of certain weaknesses in the people with whom he has dealings, and to profit himself by them; he has automatically learned to be cunning, to flatter, so to say, to stroke people the right way, and, in general, to lie.

On every convenient occasion and at every free moment he slips into a saloon or to a bar, where over a glass of beer he daydreams for hours at a time, or talks with a type like himself, or just reads the paper.

He tries to appear imposing, wears a beard, and if he is thin pads himself out to appear more important.

The totality of the manifestations of the feeling-localization in a man and the whole system of its functioning correspond perfectly to the horse of the hackney carriage in our analogy.

Incidentally, this comparison of the horse with the organization of human feeling will serve to show up particularly clearly the error and one-sidedness of the contemporary education of the rising generation.

The horse as a whole, owing to the negligence of those around it during its early years, and to its constant solitude, is as if locked up within itself; that is to say, its so to say 'inner life' is driven inside, and for external manifestions it has nothing but inertia.

Thanks to the abnormal conditions around it, the horse has never received any special education, but has been molded exclusively under the influence of constant thrashings and vile abuse.

It has always been kept tied up; and for food, instead of oats and hay, there is given to it merely straw which is utterly worthless for its real needs.

Never having seen in any of the manifestations towards it even the least love or friendliness, the horse is now ready to surrender itself completely to anybody who gives it the slightest caress.

The consequence of all this is that all the inclinations of the horse, deprived of all interests and aspirations, must inevitably be concentrated on food, drink, and the automatic yearning towards the opposite sex; hence it invariably veers in the direction where it can obtain any of these. If, for example, it catches sight of a place where even once or twice it gratified one of the enumerated needs, it waits the chance to run off in that direction.

It must further be added that although the coachman has a very feeble understanding of his duties, he can nevertheless, even though only a little, think logically; and remembering tomorrow, he either from fear of losing his job or from the desire of receiving a reward, does occasionally evince an interest in doing something or other for his employer without being driven to it; but the horse – in consequence of there not having been formed in it at the proper time, owing to the absence of any special and corresponding education, any data at all for manifesting the aspirations requisite for responsible existence – of course fails to understand (and indeed it cannot be expected that it should understand) why in general it must do anything; its obligations are therefore carried out quite inertly and only from fear of further beatings.

As far as the carriage or cart is concerned, which stands in our analogy for the body without any of the other independently formed parts of the common presence of a man, the situation is even worse.

This cart, like most carts, is made of various materials, and furthermore is of a very complicated construction.

It was designed, as is evident to every sane-thinking man, to carry all kinds of burdens, and not for the purpose for which contemporary people employ it, that is, only for carrying passengers.

The chief cause of the various misunderstandings connected with it springs from the fact that those who made the system of this cart intended it for travel on the byroads, and certain inner details of its general construction were in consequence foreseeingly made to answer to this aim.

For example, the principle of its greasing, one of the chief needs of a construction of such different materials, was so devised that the grease should spread over all the metallic parts from the shaking received from the jolts inevitable on such roads, whereas now, this cart that was designed for traveling on the byroads finds itself stationed on a rank in the city and traveling on smooth, level, asphalted roads.

In the absence of any shocks whatsoever while going along such roads, no uniform greasing of all its parts occurs, and some of them consequently must inevitably rust and cease to fulfill the action intended for them.

A cart goes easily as a rule if its moving parts are properly greased. With too little grease, these parts get heated and finally red-hot, and thus the other parts get spoiled; on the other hand, if in some part there is too much grease, the general movement of the cart is impaired, and in either case it becomes more difficult for the horse to draw it.

The contemporary coachman, our cabby neither knows nor has any suspicion of the necessity of greasing the cart, and even if he does grease it, he does so without proper knowledge, only on hearsay, blindly following the directions of the first comer.

That is why, when this cart, now adapted more or less for travel on smooth roads, has for some reason or other to go along a byroad, something always happen to it; either a nut gives way, or a bolt gets bent or something or other gets loose; and after these attempts at traveling along such roads, the journey rarely ends without more or less considerable repairs.

In any case, to make use of this cart for the purposes for which it was made is already impossible without risk. If repairs are begun, it is necessary to take the cart all to pieces, examine all its parts, and, as is done in such cases, 'kerosene' them, clean them, and put them together again; and frequently it becomes clearly necessary immediately and without fail to change a part. This is all very well if it happens to be an inexpensive part, but it may turn out to be more costly than a new cart.

And so, all that has been said about the separate parts of that organization of which, taken as a whole, a hackney carriage consists can be fully applied also to the general organization of the common presence of a man.

Owing to the absence among contemporary people of any knowledge and ability specially to prepare in a corresponding way the rising generation for responsible existence by educating all the separate parts composing their common presences, every person of today is a confused and extremely ludicrous something, that is to say, again using this example we have taken, a something resembling the following picture.

A carriage just out of the factory, made on the latest model, polished by genuine German craftsmen from the town of Barmen, and harnessed to the kind of horse which is called in the locality named Transcaucasia, a 'Dglozidzi.' ('Dzi' is a horse; 'Dgloz'is the name of a certain Armenian specialist in buying utterly worthless horses and skinning them.)

On the box of this stylish carriage sits an unshaven, unkempt, sleepy coachman-cabby, dressed in a shabby cloak which he has retrieved from the rubbish heap where it had been thrown as utterly worthless by the kitchenmaid Maggie. On his head reposes a brand-new top hat, an exact replica of Rockefeller's; and in his buttonhole there is displayed a giant chrysanthemum.

This picture, however ludicrous, of contemporary man, is an inevitable result, chiefly because from the first day of the arising and formation of a contemporary man, all these three parts formed in him – which parts, although diversely caused and with properties of diverse quality, should nevertheless, at the period of his responsible existence for pursuing a single aim, all together represent his entire whole – begin, so to say, to 'live' and to become fixed in their specific manifestations separately one from another, never having been trained either to the requisite automatic reciprocal maintenance, reciprocal assistance, or to any, even though only approximate, reciprocal understanding; and thus, when afterward concerted manifestations are required, these concerted manifestations do not appear.

Thanks to what is called the 'system of education of the rising generation' which at the present time has already been completely fixed in the life of man and which consists singly and solely in training the pupils, by means of constant repetition to the point of 'madness,' to sense various almost empty words and expressions and to recognize, only by the difference in their consonance, the reality supposed to be signified by these words and expressions, the coachman is still able to explain after a fashion the various desires arising in him, but only to types similar to his own outside of his common presence, and he is sometimes even able approximately to understand others.

This coachman-cabby of ours, gossiping with other coachmen while waiting for a fare, and sometimes, as is said, 'flirting' at the gate with the neighbor's maid, even learns various forms of what is called 'amiability.'

He also, by the way, according to the external conditions of the life of coachmen in general, gradually automatizes himself to distinguish one street from the other and to calculate, for instance, during repairs in some street, how to get to the required street from another direction.

But as for the horse, although the maleficent invention of contemporary people which is called education does not extend over the horse's formation, and in consequence its inherited possibilities are not atrophied, yet owing to the fact that this formation proceeds under the conditions of the abnormally established process of the ordinary existence of people, and that the horse grows up ignored like an orphan by everybody, and moreover an ill-treated orphan, it neither acquires anything corresponding to the established psyche of the coachman nor learns anything of what he knows, and hence is quite ignorant of all the forms of reciprocal relationship which have become usual for the coachman, and no contact is established between them for understanding each other.

It is possible, however, that in its locked-in life the horse does nevertheless learn some form of relationship with the coachman and that even, perhaps, it is familiar with some 'language'; but the trouble is, that the coachman does not know this and does not even suspect its possibility.

Apart from the fact that, owing to the said abnormal conditions, no data for even an approximate understanding of each other are formed between the horse and the coachman, there are also still other and numerous external causes, independent of them, which fail to give them the possibility of together actualizing that one purpose for which they were both destined.

The point is, that just as the separate independent parts of a 'hackney' are connected – namely, the carriage to the horse by the shafts and the horse to the coachman by reins – so also are the separate parts of the general organization of man connected with each other; namely, the body is connected to the feeling-organization by the blood, and the feeling-organization is connected to the organization actualizing the functioning of mentation or consciousness by what is called Hanbledzoin, that is, by that substance which arises in the common presence of a man from all intentionally made being-efforts.

The wrong system of education existing at the present time has led to the coachman's ceasing to have any effect whatever on his horse, unless we allow the fact that he is merely able by means of the reins to engender in the consciousness of the horse just three ideas – right, left, and stop.

Strictly speaking he cannot always do even this, because the reins in general are made of materials that react to various atmospheric phenomena: for example, during a pouring rain they swell and contract; and in heat, the contrary; thereby changing their effect upon the horse's automatized sensitiveness of perception.

The same proceeds in the general organization of the average man whenever from some impression or other the so to say 'density and tempo' of the Hanbledzoin changes in him, when his thoughts entirely lose all possibility of affecting his feeling-organization.

And so, to resume all that has been said, one must willy-nilly acknowledge that every man should strive to have his own 'I'; otherwise he will always represent a hackney carriage in which any fare can sit and which any fare can dispose of just as he pleases.

And here it will not be superfluous to point out that the Institute-for-the-Harmonious-Development-of-Man, organized on the system of Mr. Gurdjieff, has, among its fundamental tasks, also the task of on the one hand correspondingly educating in its pupils each of the enumerated independent personalities separately as well as in their general reciprocal relationship; and on the other hand of begetting and fostering in each of its pupils what every bearer of the name of 'man without quotation marks' should have – his own 'I'.[1]

13 Man's possible evolution

In order to prepare for his freedom, man must know that there are seven degrees of the possible evolution of the self. One of the causes of our blindness is that we give the word 'man' a content which, while it certainly remains vague, nevertheless makes a claim to universality. Man and mankind, when we envisage them from the philosophical angle, remain absolute concepts for us. Gurdjieff puts us on our guard against this fallacy and asks us to learn a 'new language' which contains 'hardly any new terms or new nomenclature, *but it bases the construction of speech upon a new principle, namely, the principle of relativity*'.[1]

In ordinary language, according to Gurdjieff, is found 'one of the reasons for the divergence between the line of knowledge and the line of being'.[2] It is a subjective language, unfitted for communication, whose elements at best behave, in the words of André Breton, 'like wreckage on the surface of a dead sea'. It is an imprecise language, because thought is imprecise, muddled and biased. A language so defective that it gives rise to Mullah Nassr Eddin's remark about 'grammarians' that 'All they can do is to wrangle with pigs about the quality of oranges.'[3]

Without a doubt, there is no better definition of the 'new language' seen by Gurdjieff as absolutely necessary than that given by René Daumal in the foreword to his novel *A Night of Serious Drinking* (*La Grande Beuverie*):

> Clear discourse presupposes three conditions: a speaker who knows what he wishes to say, a listener in a state of wakefulness, and a language common to both. But it is not enough for a

language to be clear in the way that an algebraic proposition is clear. It must also have a real, not simply a possible content. Before this happens, the participants must have, as a fourth element, a common experience of the thing which is spoken of. . . . But it is still not enough for language to have clarity and content, as when I say 'that day, it was raining' or 'three plus two make five'; it must also have a goal and an imperative.[4]

The goal will be to enable man to liberate himself. The imperative is that only a language of this kind makes it possible to understand the idea of *evolution*:

'The fundamental property of the new language is that *all* ideas in it are concentrated round *one* idea, . . . This idea is the idea of *evolution*. Of course, not evolution in the sense of *mechanical* evolution, because such an evolution does not exist, but in the sense of a conscious and volitional evolution, which alone is possible.'[5]

Man is alive, as the whole universe is alive. This is one of the principal laws of Gurdjieff's cosmology. Alive, that is to say endowed with consciousness, even if only in embryo.

'In speaking of evolution it is necessary to understand from the outset that no mechanical evolution is possible. The evolution of man is the evolution of his consciousness. *And "consciousness" cannot evolve unconsciously*. The evolution of man is the evolution of his will, and "will" cannot evolve involuntarily. The evolution of man is the evolution of his power of doing, and "doing" cannot be the result of things which "happen."'[6]

The ordinary man, Gurdjieff tells us, is a 'three-brained' or 'three-centred' being, which means that the functions of the human machine are shared among three centres:

1 The physical centre, itself divided into instinctive centre, moving centre and sex centre.
2 The emotional centre, seat of the emotions, the feelings.
3 The intellectual centre, seat of the mind.

If the intellectual and emotional centres are the seat of functions which have long been distinguished in the West (think for example of the Platonic νοῦς and θυμσς), Gurdjieff's analysis of the instinctive and moving functions differs appreciably from the standard accepted analyses.

In *In Search of the Miraculous*, Ouspensky recalls how man's actions used to be divided 'into "conscious" actions, "automatic" actions (which must at first be conscious), "instinctive" actions (expedient, but without consciousness of purpose), and "reflexes," simple and complex, which are never conscious and which can, in certain cases, be inexpedient'.[7]

Gurdjieff stresses our wrong use of the words 'instinct' and 'instinctive'. To the instinctive centre belong solely the functions, such as breathing, circulation of the blood and digestion, as well as the interior and exterior reflexes.

What we usually call instinct, the so-called innate tendency towards various determined actions, Gurdjieff assigns to the moving centre:

> 'The moving functions of man, as well as of animals, of a bird, of a dog, *must be learned* . . . but that which is usually explained as "instinct" is very often a series of complex moving functions which young animals learn from older ones.'[8]

Furthermore, each of the centres is autonomous, each is a 'mind' in itself. The moving and the instinctive centres have no need of the intellectual centre in order to perform their functions. The intelligence of ants, bees and termites is of a kind which stems from the moving centre, which basically works by imitation.

We ourselves are 'three-brained beings', but the abnormal feature of what happens in us is that our centres are not in balance, that we either know nothing about them, or we deny their very existence. We have no 'permanent center of gravity'. In some people the centre of gravity of their psychic life is located in the moving centre, in others it is in the emotional or the intellectual centre. Thus Gurdjieff distinguishes three basic types, whom he calls man number one, number two and number three. The knowledge of man number one, who is dependent on the moving centre, is a 'knowledge' based on imitation. Man number one is incapable of any personal thought. He clings to old ideas which he does not *understand* in any case, and behaves 'like a parrot or a monkey'.

Man number two takes an interest only in what he likes. He is the man of whims and crazes, or sometimes he is the sick man who will 'know only what he dislikes, what repels him and what evokes in him fear, horror and loathing'.[9]

Man number three is the man of theory and everlasting argument. His understanding remains necessarily literal, and his 'thinking' peters out into idle dialectics, subtle quibblings and useless systematizing. He is one of those 'Purificators of Accounts' whom René Daumal describes in *A Night of Serious Drinking*: 'Their philosopher's stone, their squared circle, which they never attain but which rules all their questing, is the perfect System which would apply to no human experience and remain eminently unusable.'[10]

All men belong to one or another of these categories. Yet man can perfect himself. He can first of all become conscious of his 'mechanicalness', stop asserting the unity of his I, freely set himself goals. Such a man finds himself on the threshold of the 'esoteric circle' and he escapes much of the hazard of the Circle of the Confusion of Tongues. If 'mechanical' mankind may be symbolized by the figure of the *hidden dragon* (which I borrow from Taoism), man number four would be symbolized by the *dragon rampant*. In man number four the centres are beginning to be balanced. But Gurdjieff reminds us that man number four 'is always *the product of school work*', which explains his rarity. 'He has a *permanent center of gravity* which consists in his ideas, in his valuation of the work, and in his relation to the school.'[11]

As well as the centres already defined, there are two other centres in man, which Gurdjieff calls the *higher emotional centre* and the *higher thinking centre*. In all men these centres exist, *fully developed*, and always working correctly. It is the lower centres, which work badly, which we have to act upon. But we can only benefit from the work of the higher centres by our own *conscious* efforts: in ordinary life they are inaccessible to us, except at rare brief moments which are usually erased from our memory. Gurdjieff tells us that it is sometimes possible to connect with the higher thinking centre through the higher emotional centre:

'It is only from descriptions of mystical experiences, ecstatic states, and so on, that we know cases of such connections. These states can occur on the basis of religious emotions, or, for short moments, through particular narcotics; or in certain pathological states such as epileptic fits or accidental traumatic injuries to the brain, in which cases it is difficult to say which is the cause and which is the effect, that is, whether the pathological state results from this connection or is its cause.'[12]

Neither man number one, nor man number two, nor man number three is able to use his higher centres. Man number four has this ability, because he knows 'whither he is going'. His is the way of voluntary suffering and conscious efforts.

'Man number five has already been crystallized; he cannot change as man number one, two, and three change.'[13]

The multiple 'I's are unified. Man number five has developed his 'astral body'; in him the *higher emotional centre* is functioning. In Taoist symbolism, he is the *dragon leaping*. Consciousness of himself is, with unity, his principal attribute. 'What he knows, the whole of him knows.'[14]

Man number six accedes to 'objective consciousness'. His knowledge 'is the complete knowledge possible to man'. He is the *dragon flying*, and in him the *higher intellectual centre* functions. But Gurdjieff points out that his knowledge 'can still be lost'.[15]

What characterizes man number seven is the permanence of his I; 'The knowledge of man number seven in his own knowledge, which cannot be taken away from him; it is the *objective* and completely *practical* knowledge of *All*.'[16]

Men numbers one, two and three constitute the Circle of the Confusion of Tongues, and are obviously the most numerous. Man number four stands on the threshold, on the boundary between the Circle of the Confusion of Tongues and the esoteric circles. There are three of these: the esoteric circle proper, to which man number seven belongs; the mesoteric circle, the domain of man number six; and the exoteric circle, the seat of man number five. To each of these circles there corresponds a *language*, and in each of these circles all men speak the *same* language. Initiation means learning the language of a circle higher than one's own present one, and learning it not only according to the line of knowledge but also according to the line of being. It is nowhere near enough to know the system intellectually. He must understand things 'with his whole mass', and any such understanding is bound to produce great sufferings.

But how does a person acquire experimental knowledge of the working of the human machine? It can only be done through the assiduous practice of self-observation, and this may take on two aspects:

'There are two methods of self-observation: *analysis*, or attempts at analysis, that is, attempts to find the answers to the questions: upon what does a certain thing depend, and why does it happen; and the second method is registering, simply *recording* in one's mind what is observed at the moment.'[17]

Self-observation first involves taking a number of 'mental photographs' of oneself, without any self-indulgence. At least in the first phase, which may be fairly prolonged, the work of analysis is not at all desirable. Let us learn to recognize the work of given centres in ourselves, and especially the wrong work of centres, because it happens too often that one of the centres usurps the functions of another. For instance, the emotional centre will manifest itself at moments when only the intellectual centre should be working, and 'brings unnecessary nervousness, feverishness, and hurry, into situations where, on the contrary, calm judgment and deliberation are essential'.[18]

Let us also recall that whenever we parrot other people's thinking, not out of any real necessity but solely for the sake of display, it is not our intellectual centre which is functioning, but our moving centre. Similar instances could easily be accumulated. One of the best images to enable us to understand the gravity of this wrong work of centres is provided by Gurdjieff to illustrate the fact that: 'The mind cannot understand shades of feeling.'

'We shall see this clearly', he said, 'if we imagine one man reasoning about the emotions of another. He is not feeling anything himself so the feelings of another do not exist for him. *A full man does not understand a hungry one.* But for the other *they have a very definite existence.* And the decisions of the first, that is of the mind, can never satisfy him.'[19]

For the judicious conduct of self-observation it is also necessary, as it were, to stand outside ourselves, to become aware of what we are *in reality*, contrasting that ill-defined I with the protean 'I' that bears our name:

'A man must realize that he indeed consists of two men.

'One is the man he calls "I" and whom others call "Ouspensky," "Zakharov," or "Petrov." The other is the real *he*, the real *I*, which appears in his life only for very short moments and which can become firm and permanent only after a very lengthy period of work.'[20]

In ordinary life we are not ourselves but that false and tyrannical 'Ouspensky', 'Zakharov' or 'Petrov', because we incessantly play a part, and we utterly lack *sincerity*. Not that we necessarily tell lies in a conscious manner, but we lie each time we talk about things we know nothing of, and can know nothing of. *He*, this person we embody, must become our *enemy*. For we are his slaves. It is always *he* who asserts himself, whereas *I* can never do what I want. But it would be an error to pass any judgment arising out of this self-observation. To baptize as 'Zakharov' the 'I' we do not like, and as 'I' the one who gratifies us, is to allow Zakharov to judge himself. Often what we reckon as positive in ourselves is in fact negative. We identify ourselves with our ideals, but these ideals are not of our own making, and are arbitrarily defined. I like philosophy because I have always been told that it was the highest form of learning, and I aspire to become a philosopher. Observing myself in accordance with the method described by Gurdjieff, I conclude that when I try my hand at pondering, my true 'I' is asserting itself, whereas the exact opposite may be the case, and my true 'I' only aspires to activities which in my blindness I consider as 'menial'. A great deal of patience and lucidity are necessary if we want to free the true 'I' from the chains loaded on to it by the 'personage' who dominates us. Furthermore, we keep identifying ourselves with some particular self-image which appeals to us. When people observe identification in themselves 'they consider it a very good trait and call it "enthusiasm," "zeal," "passion," "spontaneity," "inspiration," and names of that kind'.[21] Very seldom do we form an image of ourselves which is devoid of self-indulgence; hardly anybody volunteers to play the game of severity, which all too often is falsely accused of harshness or callousness. This is one of the reasons why Gurdjieff's teaching has sometimes been given such a poor reception. There is no place for sentimentality if we are to accomplish the austere work upon ourselves which is required of us. Indulgence is not love but short-sightedness in a being.

'Identifying' may assume another form, which Gurdjieff calls 'considering'. Sometimes a man attaches inordinate importance to other people's opinion of himself, sometimes to the opinion he himself holds – or thinks he ought to hold – of others. In the first case his relations with others bear the stamp of suspicion, resentment and acrimony; in the other, that of weakness and 'bad conscience'. In both cases he is 'considering' realities which are not worth considering. Just as he gave his various other weaknesses high-flown names, so he calls these manifestations of his own power-lessness 'sincerity', and refuses to resist them for fear of 'diminish-ing' or 'impoverishing' himself.

Gurdjieff draws a contrast between what he calls internal 'con-sidering' and the *external* considering which is 'adaptation towards people, to their understanding, to their requirements'. It 'requires a knowledge of men, an understanding of their tastes, habits, and prejudices'. Lastly it requires 'a great power over oneself, a great control over oneself'.[22]

It is the defective 'I' in us, our 'Ouspensky', our 'Zakharov' or our 'Petrov', which sometimes 'identifies' and sometimes 'considers' faultily – in a word it is our *personality* which goes astray.

Gurdjieff said:

> 'It must be understood that man consists of two parts: *essence* and *personality*. Essence in man is what is *his own*. Personality in man is what is "not his own." . . . Essence is the truth in man; personality is the false.'[23]

Usually we know nothing of our own essence, and identify with our personality, which after all is considerably developed, whereas our essence may have stopped growing very early. 'As a rule man's essence is either primitive, savage, and childish, or else simply stupid. The development of essence depends on work on oneself.'[24]

In fact, essence seldom reaches a satisfactory level of growth. Often it stops growing very soon, and it is the personality that stifles it. Gurdjieff asserts that it is possible to convince oneself of the relation between essence and personality by subjecting people to hypnotic experiments, or administering 'certain narcotics'.

'Narcotics' is the word used in *In Search of the Miraculous*, but it is a word which belongs to the vocabulary of Ouspensky, not the lan-guage of Gurdjieff. At the beginning of the book, Ouspensky says to Gurdjieff: 'There are substances which yogis take to induce certain states. Might these not be, in certain cases, narcotics?' Gurdjieff answers:

> 'In many cases these substances are *those which you call "narcotics"* [my emphasis]. . . . There are schools which make use of narcotics in the right way. People in these schools take them for self-study; in order to take a look ahead, to know their possibilities

better, to see beforehand, "in advance," what can be attained
later on as the result of prolonged work.'[25]

These 'narcotics' might be the *iboga* of the Africans or the *peyotl* of
the Mexican Indians, for example – substances which Charles Duits
would call 'the consciousness illuminators',[26] or, to discard the
pejorative character of the commonly accepted terms, 'lucidogens':

> I do not become other when I 'eat the acrimonious', I become
> myself. The 'dark period' is dark because I am afraid of losing
> myself. It comes to an end when I find out that it is the exact
> opposite which is happening. I am not losing myself, I am losing
> my limitations. This loss is sometimes harrowing if I believe that
> the limitations (mistaken convictions, scientific, philosophic or
> conformist ideas) are my personality, sublime if I understand that
> I am 'in my heart of hearts' the Tao, God, the One and only, the
> Void, Brahman, the Tathagata – and all the intermediary 'states
> of consciousness' and 'infra-human states' as well.[27]

What I discover by removing from my 'ordinary waking consciousness' the deposits encrusted upon it by all my 'mistaken
convictions' is my essence. And the more 'cultured' I am, the more
suffocating these 'convictions' are for my true 'I', and the feebler my
essence. Whereas: 'Essence has more chances of development in
men who live nearer to nature in difficult conditions of constant
struggle and danger.'[28]

Not that we have to condemn everything in man which derives
from the personality: without education, without culture, there
could be no progress either. But it is right for essence and personality to develop in step with each other, and: 'A man's real *I*, his
individuality, can grow only from his essence.'[29]

14 The traditional ways and the way of the 'sly man'

Gurdjieff teaches that there are four ways leading to immortality, four ways through which man can acquire the Individuality, Consciousness and Will without which the freedom he claims to enjoy, and his alleged capacity for *doing*, are illusory.

Among these ways, three are traditional. Gurdjieff calls them the way of the fakir, the way of the monk and the way of the yogi.

We have seen that man has the possibility of possessing four bodies. Gurdjieff asks us to imagine a house with four rooms. Man lives in it, crammed lop-sidedly into the shabbiest, most dilapidated room, and usually is either unaware that the others exist, or knows that they do, but does not have the key to them.

The shabby room which man occupies is his 'planetary body'. The other rooms, full of treasures, are the 'higher being bodies'. And it is when he enters the fourth room that man reaches immortality.

'The way of the fakir is the way of struggle with the physical body, the way of work on the first room.'[1]

The fakir ruthlessly mortifies his body and imposes real tortures on himself in order to strengthen his own will – will of a 'physical' kind, says Gurdjieff, through which he may some day gain access to the fourth room and attain 'the possibility of forming the fourth body'. 'But his other functions – emotional, intellectual, and so forth – remain undeveloped.'[2]

The development of these functions becomes possible only if the fakir, once he has acquired his strength, is taught and helped by 'schools of yogis'.

The way of the fakir is perhaps the harshest and most painful of all. It demands such mortifications and such great feats from the adept that eventually he is nothing but a block of brute will-power.

The way of the monk is 'the way of faith, the way of religious feeling, and of sacrifice'. All his work 'is concentrated on the second room, on the second body, that is, on *feelings*'.[3] It is the way of fervour and emotional outpouring, but it is also the way of penance and of incessant struggle against oneself.

What the monk acquires in the long run is *unity*, 'will over the emotions'. He too can reach the fourth room, 'but his physical body and his thinking capacities may remain undeveloped'.[4] To secure their development, 'fresh sacrifices, fresh hardships, fresh renunciations' are necessary. As Gurdjieff stresses, '*a monk has to become a yogi and a fakir.*'[5]

The way of the yogi 'is the way of knowledge, the way of mind,'[6] the way of work on the third room. It has the advantage over the other two ways that the adept is aware of his degree of development. His work leads him up to the fourth room, but it remains for him to 'gain the mastery over his body and emotions'.[7] This is no easy matter, but there is no doubt that his is a less painful way than the monk's or the fakir's of achieving that balance of the centres without which no final crystallization of the 'I' can come about.

Fakir, monk and yogi are undoubtedly travelling – one barefoot, the second shod, the third perhaps on a donkey – but all three have to realize at the end of their road that they have forgotten some essential luggage. And they must necessarily retrace their steps and start again, often a great many times, before being finally able to know immortality at the end of their journey.

The relationship with the teacher also varies according to the way adopted.

While the fakir is content to *imitate* the teacher, who is no more than a model with whom the imitator does not maintain any real relationship, the monk must instead have 'absolute faith' in the teacher, for the monk's way is the way of *obedience*. As for the yogi, he partly imitates and partly *obeys* the teacher (with an obedience exalted by faith), but there comes a point when he takes leave of the teacher in order to become his own master. Gurdjieff concludes:

> 'But all the ways, the way of the fakir as well as the way of the monk and the way of the yogi, have one thing in common. They all begin with the most difficult thing, with a complete change of life, with a renunciation of all worldly things. A man must give up

his home, his family if he has one, renounce all the pleasures, attachments, and duties of life, and go out into the desert, or into a monastery or a yogi school.'

What the traditional ways have in common, he goes on, is that they are ways of sacrifice: 'From the very first day, from the very first step on his way, [the follower] must die to the world; only thus can he hope to attain anything on one of these ways.'[8]

In addition, these ways are all 'tied to permanent forms',[9] in other words to religions. Adopting them means making an act of faith. Inasmuch as they are tied to particular religious systems their drawback is that they may not be appropriate for the doubters that we in the West have generally become. The sacrifice they require as a *necessary preliminary* may either appear hazardous or else is no longer possible.

From another angle, since each of the ways corresponds to one of the three basic human types, a 'man number four', who possesses a permanent centre of gravity, and whose three centres have begun to be balanced, is bound to renounce choosing any given one, since he at once detects its inadequacies, and even perhaps its relative absurdity.

But there is, says Gurdjieff, a fourth way. It is the way of work on the three rooms, that is the three centres, simultaneously. This kind of work is possible because the man following the fourth way possesses 'certain knowledge' available to neither the fakir, the monk, nor the yogi; he knows a *secret* which they do not know. That is why 'the fourth way is sometimes called *the way of the sly man*'.[10]

'How the "sly man" learned this secret, it is not known. Perhaps he found it in some old books, perhaps he inherited it, perhaps he bought it, perhaps he stole it from someone. It makes no difference. The "sly man" knows the secret and with its help outstrips the fakir, the monk, and the yogi.'[11]

Clearly the 'sly man' is shrouded in mystery. Nobody can understand him without himself being a 'sly man'. Others lose themselves in conjecture, or become angry about an ease which bothers them and which in their jealous ignorance they are tempted to ascribe to some devilry.

The fourth way 'demands no renunciation'. 'On the contrary,' says Gurdjieff, 'the conditions of life in which a man is placed at the beginning of his work, in which, so to speak, the work finds him, are the *best possible* for him, at any rate at the beginning of the work.'[12]

Let us suppose that the men of any of these four ways have one and the same end in view. To reach it, says Gurdjieff, if it takes the fakir 'a whole month of intense torture', the monk must impose on himself 'a week of fasting, continual prayer, privations, and penance' and the yogi a day's work on the intellectual centre. As for the man on the fourth way, he 'knows quite definitely what substances he needs for his aims and he knows that these substances can be produced within the body by a month of physical suffering, by a week of emotional strain, or by a day of mental exercises – and also, *that they can be introduced into the organism from without if it is known how to do it.*'[13]

Teaching and initiation may assume many forms on the fourth way. 'There are no institutions connected with it.'[14]

It is, in other words, always *adapted*.

That is why schools or groups, in a word, what Gurdjieff called 'the work', only exist for a time. There can be no question of subordinating one's entire life to it. Not that the work ceases, but it changes its nature. There is a moment when a man must necessarily take his leave, cut his moorings, become a teacher himself. Moreover, in the group, everyone is teacher, and everyone is pupil. Each time a man 'takes a step up' he must place another man on the step he has left.

'A man may attain something, for instance, some special powers, and may later on sacrifice these powers in order to raise other people to his level. If the people with whom he is working ascend to his level, he will receive back all that he has sacrificed. But if they do not ascend, he may lose it altogether.'[15]

Inside a group or school there are different circles. One of the most common mistakes is to believe, at the beginning of the work, that one is bound to benefit from the help of a teacher of the highest level.

'Usually the man himself is not worth a brass farthing, but he must have as teacher no other than Jesus Christ. To less he will not agree. And it never enters his head that even if he were to meet such a teacher as Jesus Christ, taking him as he is described in the Gospels, he would never be able to follow him because it would be necessary to be on the level of an apostle in order to be a pupil of

Jesus Christ. Here is a definite law. The higher the teacher, the more difficult for the pupil.'[16]

Thus the disciple encounters not one teacher but as many teachers as he ascended 'steps' on the 'stairway' that leads to the way. This begins only 'after the *last threshold* on the stairway, on a level much higher than the ordinary level of life'.[17] The first step simply represents 'the moment when the man who is looking for the way meets a man who knows the way'.[18]

It takes an enormous amount of work before a man can even claim to be travelling. For instead of toiling along the road and having to retrace his steps so as to pick up forgotten luggage, the 'sly man' contrives to cover the whole journey without a single halt. At the moment of entering upon the fourth way, the road becomes, if not easy, then at least fast. The most painful and troublesome are the preparations. They can take years. But once he finds himself on the way, the man is, so to speak, transfigured. Something inside him has been settled. For one thing, he knows where he is going, and 'even if he leaves the way, he will be unable to return to where he started from'.[19]

Whichever way he follows, in the work a man escapes from the *law of accident*. When he is subject to that law, the influences he undergoes are 'created *in life itself* or by life itself. Influences of race, nation, country, climate, family, education, society, profession, manners and customs, wealth, poverty, current ideas, and so on.'[20]

There is a passage in *Beelzebub's Tales* where Gurdjieff illustrates this fact with an image:

> 'A man comes into the world like a clean sheet of paper, which immediately all around him begin vying with each other to dirty and fill up with education, morality, the information we call knowledge, and with all kinds of feelings of duty, honor, conscience, and so on and so forth. . . .
>
> 'The sheet of paper gradually becomes dirty, and the dirtier it becomes, that is to say, the more a man is stuffed with ephemeral information and those notions of duty, honor, and so on which are dinned into him or suggested to him by others, the "cleverer" and worthier is he considered by those around him.'[21]

Gurdjieff contrasts these accidental and harmful influences with those 'created consciously by conscious men for a definite purpose', adding that: 'Influences of this kind are usually embodied in the form of religious systems and teachings, philosophical doctrines, works of art, and so on.'[22]

But these influences, which are good ones, quickly become distorted, because they are badly transmitted or badly interpreted, or because they are caught up 'into the general vortex of life' and in the long run there is nothing left to distinguish them from influences of the first kind.

Anyone who wants to be freed from his own mechanicalness must first learn to 'separate the two kinds of influences'. Mind and heart should allow him to achieve this. A point is reached, says Gurdjieff, when a man *remembers* and *feels* influences of the second kind 'with his whole mass'. At that point 'they form within him a kind of *magnetic center*, which begins to attract to itself kindred influences and in this manner it grows'.[23]

Influences of the second kind derive from a centre which lies outside life – meaning ordinary life – and which Gurdjieff calls the esoteric centre.

A 'man in life', if he is capable of distinguishing influences of the first kind from the second, is also capable of recognizing a man who knows the way when he meets him – the man who is linked directly or indirectly, with the esoteric centre from which comes all that makes up the magnetic centre. In so far as he listens to the man he has recognized, at that moment he finds himself subject to a new and 'conscious' influence, which is also *direct*. It is at that moment that the work may truly begin (see Fig. 14.1).

But it can happen that the magnetic centre is wrongly formed, and that the man confuses influences belonging to different domains, or else that he has distorted 'the traces of influences of the second kind'[25] through his own ignorance or arrogance.

Such a man can only nurture false ideas, is incapable of choosing himself a teacher, and it may even be that the 'will to power' will lead him to deceive others deliberately.

The man who sets out or wishes to set out along the fourth way already possesses a strong magnetic centre. He has been able to recognize the teacher's voice wherever it may have been raised. If he has not practised traditional ways then at least he has pondered upon them at length. He is a disappointed man, disappointed by the rigidity and narrowness of the systems he knows. Gurdjieff said:

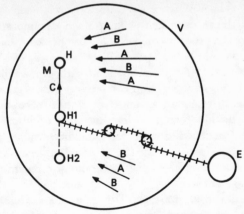

V ... life
H ... an individual man
A ... influences created in life, that is, in life itself—the first kind of influences
B ... influences created outside life but thrown into the general vortex of
        life—the second kind of influences
H1 ... a man, connected by means of succession with the esoteric centre or
        pretending to it
E ... esoteric centre, standing outside the general laws of life
M ... magnetic centre in man
C ... influence of man *h*1 on man *h*; in the event of his actually being connected
        with the esoteric centre, directly or by succession, this is the third kind of
        influence. This influence is conscious and under its action at the point *m*,
        that is, in the magnetic centre, a man becomes free from the law of accident
H2 ... a man, deceiving himself or deceiving others and having no connection,
        either directly or by succession, with the esoteric centre.

Figure 14.1 [24]

'A man cannot feel what is most valuable in the system unless he
is disappointed in what he has been doing, disappointed in what
he has been searching for. . . . But you must understand what this
means. I say for instance that a religious man should be disappointed in religion. This does not mean that he should lose his
faith. On the contrary, it means being "disappointed" *in the teaching and the methods only*.[26]

Gurdjieff's teaching belongs to the order of the fourth way. This
teaching is not just embodied in books, but above all in the work of a
certain number of groups.
'One man can do nothing'; he cannot awaken himself. The work

of groups, which is far from being a purely intellectual task, is necessary. But to describe this kind of work is impossible. All that can be formulated are a certain number of rules without which no group could exist.

First: 'No work of groups is possible without a teacher. The work of groups with a wrong teacher can produce only negative results.'[27]

Next, it is essential to understand 'the necessary balancing principle', the aim 'without which the work could not exist'.[28] But this kind of understanding is not immediate, and demands much effort.

Then again, it is necessary to submit without reservation to a number of conditions.

The first is to keep secret all that one learns. Not that there is anything really hermetic about what is taught in the group, but the novice cannot hope to convey what he hears correctly, even supposing that he understands it. Gurdjieff adds that there is another and no less important reason:

'It is very difficult for a man to keep silent about things that
interest him. He would like to speak about them to everyone with
whom he is accustomed to share his thoughts, as he calls it. This is
the most mechanical of all desires and in this case silence is the
most difficult abstinence of all.'[29]

The second requirement is to tell the truth with a sincerity which is not just spontaneous (and in any case illusory) but *cultivated*: the very fact that I forget, if I do forget, means that I do not dare to say it.

The third requirement is to remember why one comes to the group. One comes as much to learn as to work, but Gurdjieff reminds us that we are to learn and work not necessarily in the way that might suit us, but in accordance with the instructions of the teacher, who alone knows our needs.

Lastly, to work: not just to be satisfied with attending the group, but to *work*. Work of this kind demands obedience to rules. In the work, every rule is an *aid* for the disciple, and these rules 'can never be either easy, pleasant, or comfortable. On the contrary, they ought to be difficult, unpleasant, and uncomfortable; otherwise they would not answer their purpose. Rules are the alarm clocks which wake the sleeping man.'[30]

We move like ghosts. None of our actions is the fruit of a considered will. All our gestures have something jerky and inharmonious about them. We pay no attention to things. Neither the grain of this paper nor the coolness of that glass affect us. And we pass by other ghosts, with worn-out faces, whose twisted skeletons creak within the flesh. We are haggard, crooked, putrefying. We wear absurd clothes, and wear them without elegance. And we think. Or rather, images flit about in our heads, memories, obsessions. Even supposing that we do claim to be happy, it is the happiness of pigs in a wallow. Sometimes a few sparks flare in the night of our consciousness. We are assailed by vertigo, and make haste to forget them. We have love and respect neither for earth nor sky. We make use of objects without seeing that we are mishandling them. Go into a restaurant and watch the men and women who would set up such a howl if somebody were to assert their absence of consciousness. Forks and spoons are lifted towards mouths which open mechanically. Do they even know what they are eating – leaf, root, slice of dead animal? It is enough for it to be 'good' – no, not even that, for it to be 'edible' – and decomposing flesh cooked and re-cooked in stale oils slides into the stomach. Let anyone who lays claim to consciousness at least have the grace not to bolt his food down like an animal: at that moment I might be able to believe him.

To begin with, at least, it is the purpose of the work to enable us to escape from this hypnotic state. When I know that here, now, I am Myself, I can no longer remain on bad terms with my surroundings.

To wake and to remain awake, in order to free oneself of the countless hindrances that prevent *self-remembering*, are the first goals. There are other, less accessible, goals which only a knowledge of the 'system' – not an intellectual but a 'being' knowledge – can enable us to imagine.

15   The Law of Three

It is impossible to give a full account of Gurdjieff's cosmology in just a few pages, particularly because this cosmology cannot be entirely understood by *one man alone* – for proof, read *Beelzebub's Tales*. For anybody who wanted to draw upon the whole of its resources it would be necessary to constitute a group such as those mentioned by Gurdjieff in his books (for example the 'Society of Akhaldans', a community of Truth Seekers).* In any case it is obvious that both in his writings and in his oral teaching Gurdjieff proceeds in the manner of the 'Adherents-of-Legominism' whose activities he describes in Chapter 30 of the *Tales*. One of their spokesmen, 'the great Aksharpanziar', expressed himself as follows:

> 'In all the productions which we shall intentionally create . . . we shall intentionally introduce certain also lawful inexactitudes, and in these lawful inexactitudes we shall place, by means available to us, the contents of some true knowledge or other which is already in the possession of men of the present time.'**[1]

What I can propose is, like Ouspensky and Maurice Nicoll, only on a simpler, more modest scale than theirs, to attempt to set out a few of the fundamental aspects of this cosmology (although I shall certainly make use of their remarkable studies).

---

* Gurdjieff's main account of this Society is in Book One of *Beelzebub's Tales*, particularly pp. 211 ff. and 292 ff. On p. 297 Gurdjieff writes: 'By the word Akhaldan the following conception was then expressed: "The striving to become aware of the sense and aim of the Being of beings." ' (Tr.)

** This time is situated several centuries BC.

The fundamental and very traditional idea is that 'man is an image of the world',[2] a microcosm subject to the same laws as the macrocosm in which he appears. Those two laws, from which nothing created is exempt, are the law of Triamazikamno (Law of Three) and of Heptaparaparshinokh (Law of Seven, or Law of Octaves).

The Law of Three postulates that every phenomenon, wherever it occurs, results from the meeting of three different and opposing forces or principles. Gurdjieff observes that science realizes the existence of two of these forces: 'positive and negative magnetism, positive and negative electricity, male and female cells, and so on'.[3] But we do not know and are incapable of detecting the third force, without which nothing that is could be manifested. In the *Tales*,[4] Gurdjieff calls these forces or principles:

1 Holy-Affirming.
2 Holy-Denying.
3 Holy-Reconciling.

In Ouspensky they are referred to as active or positive, passive or negative, and neutralizing force.[5] They can also be defined by the terms *impulsion*, *resistance* and *mediation*.

In ordinary circumstances we are blind to the existence of these forces, particularly, as I say, of the third force. A man can only recognize them if he carries out intensive work on himself. Certainly if he was capable of contemplating his surroundings he would apprehend its ceaseless working. But he is so thoroughly absentminded that he is scarcely able to focus his attention on himself. As he is subject to the same laws as the universe, through *self-observation* he can learn to recognize the action of these laws in the course of his own life.

Recalling the distinction which has been drawn between essence and personality, it may be said that life itself plays the part of the third force when the personality is active and the essence passive. If a man is no longer satisfied with 'life' in all its unalterable haphazardness, and if he decided to devote himself to what Gurdjieff called the work, then the work plays the part of the third force, the essence becomes active, the personality passive. Similarly, if the active is what we want, and the passive is what puts up resistance to our wishes, when only these two forces are in play they cancel each other out, and a man chases rainbows all his life, and cannot master his fate. The third force may appear in this case in the form of a *new knowledge* enabling the man to create something new in himself.

Other images have been suggested to illustrate the role of the third force. In a pair of scales, it would be the beam. If we imagine a windmill, the wind plays the part of the active principle, the building that of the passive principle, and the sails which make a creative relation between the pressure of the wind and the resistance of the building represent the reconciling principle.[6] These images, crude as they may be, nevertheless highlight the indispensable nature of the neutralizing force. Then there is the image of bread: to make it you need flour and water, but also fire.

We have to envisage the fact that in the whole of nature, at every level, and in the vastness of the planetary worlds, the three forces are at work. Nothing can exist outside of their conjunction.

Each of these conjunctions is called a triad, and one triad leads to another, both vertically, as we shall see, in the hierarchy of creation, and horizontally in the temporal order. Each triad can in fact engender another, and it is always from the third force that the new triad arises. And what we sometimes call the 'chain of events' is but a succession of triads.

It should be added that forces are only active, passive or neutralizing in the relation they hold at a given moment, and that each of these forces may play the part of the active force in certain circumstances.

While self-study alone enables the third force to be grasped in any but an abstract manner (and any such abstract knowledge would lead nowhere), nevertheless the existence of the third force has always been attested by a great many theological or cosmogonic teachings.

It is just as much the indivisible Christian Trinity as the Hindu Trimurti. But the three forces here are manifested in the Absolute and 'possess a full and independent will, full consciousness, full understanding of themselves and of everything they do'.[7] God may appear in a sense as the original Triad, without being thereby reducible to the notion of Trinity. It is to the extent that he is creator that he manifests a threefold nature. But beyond the created worlds there is a region of being, incomprehensible to us, which is the sphere of the transcendent Absolute, not manifested, not differentiated, limitless and not to be grasped by the mind. 'As hidden, God is creator', said the thirteenth-century Sufi philosopher Ibn Arabi; 'as revealed, He is created.'

The idea of world is, like the idea of man, a relative one.

For us, the world is first of all the world of men, of mankind. But it is also the world of organic life on earth, and the earth itself. For the earth, the world is the world of the planets, and for the planets as a whole it is the solar system. For the sun it is the world of 'all suns', the Milky Way, 'an accumulation of a vast number of solar systems'.

> 'Furthermore, from an astronomical point of view, it is quite possible to presume a multitude of worlds existing at enormous distances from one another in the space of "all worlds." These worlds taken together will be "world" for the Milky Way.
>
> 'Further, passing to philosophical conclusions, we may say that "all worlds" must form some, for us, incomprehensible and unknown *Whole* or *One* (as an apple is one). This Whole, or One, or *All*, which may be called the "Absolute," or the "Independent" because, including everything within itself, it is not dependent upon anything, is "world" for "all worlds."'[8]

The ultimate world represented by the Absolute can be depicted by a circle containing a multitude of other circles, all of them concentric, symbolizing the created worlds.

Any of the rays of the great circle will display the worlds in their hierarchy.

Absolute	I
All worlds	3
All suns	6
Sun	12
All planets	24
Earth	48
Moon	96

Gurdjieff called this schema 'the ray of creation', and said that it 'is for us the "world" in the widest sense of the term'.[9] And this world in its turn is only one of countless possible worlds, which nevertheless are all ordered in the same way.

The Absolute for any world is the original creative Triad. In it the three forces are united. To it is assigned the figure 1.

It is succeeded by world 3, the world of 'all worlds', where the forces are already divided.

From this world there proceeds a further world, now subject to six laws, the world of 'all suns'. Three of the laws which rule it derive from the higher world, and three are its own.

So the process of differentiation goes on, three new laws being added to the sum of all the rest on each level.

The following world is subject to twelve laws. It is the world of our own sun. Then, under the sway of twenty-four laws, comes the world of the planets. After this we find the earth, ruled by forty-eight laws. Finally, on the last step in the scale, we find the moon, where the number of laws increases again and goes up to ninety-six.

Thus the universe is seen as a succession of triads each engendering the next. Among the worlds there is only one, world 3, which obeys the immediate will of the Absolute.

'In world 3 the Absolute creates, as it were, a general plan of all the rest of the universe, which is then further developed mechanically. The will of the Absolute cannot manifest itself in subsequent worlds apart from this plan.[10]

Each world is a *living being*, Gurdjieff remarks. The moon is not the dead world it is imagined to be, but

'one that is, so to speak, being born. It is becoming warm gradually and in time (given a favorable development of the ray of creation) it will become like the earth and have a satellite of its own, a new moon. A new link will have been added to the ray of creation. The earth, too, is not getting colder, it is getting warmer, and may in time become like the sun.'[11]

We return now to man. Living on the earth, he is subject to forty-eight orders of laws, but not all these laws are derived from the earth, and there are some which belong to higher worlds. To be free of terrestrial laws and to submit *voluntarily* to higher influences must be his goal. It is possible that he may do this, climb the ladder of realities, move on to worlds dependent on ever fewer laws and gain increasing freedom. Or, on the other hand, it may happen that by letting himself go he will find himself subject no longer to the forty-eight laws of the earth, but to the ninety-six of the moon.

Among the influences acting upon men there are good ones and less good ones. The laws are not all of the same quality. The essential thing is for man to submit to the better influences, all the more so because his position on the next to lowest level of the ray of creation is not an enviable one. But while this ascent may be possible it is not necessary, or even *natural*. Man as man has no importance: he is important only in so far as – like the plants and the animals – he plays, in relation to the worlds as a whole, a certain part whose nature I shall disclose below, but for which consciousness is not absolutely necessary.

Knowing the existence of the Law of Three enables a man to perfect himself, but this knowledge ought not to remain purely intellectual. It is most of all in the course of life that he must learn to study its action. Usually we can only recognize one of these forces, sometimes two, never or very seldom the third, and then by chance. For the forces manifested in us constantly change their nature. Sometimes we love a thing, and sometimes we hate it: our love is 'mechanical' and easily turns to hatred, as does trust to suspicion, faith to doubt, hope to despair.

If a man wants to learn to recognize the three forces he has to do something, and to do it he has to want to do it, and want it *sincerely*.

On the other hand, once he has chosen his goal he must clearly envisage all the obstacles which the second force will throw up. Then, if he is content with something other than empty words, that goal may possibly seem unattainable.

He will now set himself aims which are less sublime than he might have wished.

If he wants nothing, the second force does not appear. If he does not know what he wants, the first force remains unknown. But if he knows what he wants, and he is not just chasing wild geese, the third force may reveal itself.

That force is the overheard remark that bowls me over, opening doors on which, until now, I have been knocking in vain. It is the encounter I no longer hoped for, the encouragement I did not expect, the love or friendship without which I would fall to earth. It is the tree that speaks to me of God, the bird whose flight sets me at rest, the music that gladdens my spirit. It is that book, that stone, that sound, that colour. It is Eternity present in a grain of sand.

16   The Law of Seven

From the Absolute, the original Triad, all realities proceed. But their sequence is not the fruit of chance. The order in which they appear is determined by the fundamental Cosmic Law of Heptaparaparshinokh, or Law of Seven. This law, says Gurdjieff, like the Law of Three, requires no proving. It simply is.

Gurdjieff asserts that the universe *consists of vibrations*:

'These . . . proceed in kinds, aspects and densities of the matter which constitutes the universe, from the finest to the coarsest; they issue from various sources and proceed in various directions, crossing one another, colliding, strengthening, weakening, arresting one another, and so on.'[1]

Modern science regards these vibrations as continuous, 'proceeding uninterruptedly, ascending or descending so long as there continues to act the force of the original impulse which caused the vibration and which overcomes the resistance of the medium in which the vibrations proceed'.[2] Gurdjieff says – and this is the basis of the Law of Seven: 'In this instance the view of ancient knowledge is opposed to that of contemporary science because at the base of the understanding of vibrations ancient knowledge places the principle of the *discontinuity of vibrations*.'[3]

The vibrations, like water moving along a pipe which narrows at certain points, slow down at intervals.

Envisaging a vibration whose frequency doubles, there are two such points. If we imagine a diagram showing the shift from a frequency of 1,000 to 2,000 a second, Gurdjieff states that according to ancient science the line drawn is 'divided into *eight* unequal steps corresponding to the rate of increase in the vibrations', the period being called an *octave* or eighth.

'In the guise of this formula ideas of the octave have been handed down from teacher to pupil, from one school to another. In very remote times one of these schools found that it was possible to apply this formula to music.'[4]

In the musical scale we therefore possess a symbolic representation of the Law of Seven.

If we take the ascending octave, along which the vibrations double their frequency, and designate the starting point by the note *do*, to reach the *do* of the next octave the intervening period is divided into eight unequal parts, 'because the frequency of vibrations does not increase uniformly'.[5]

But the diagrammatic representation takes no account of the inequality of the parts:

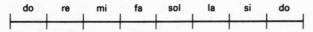

| do | re | mi | fa | sol | la | si | do |

'The ratio of the pitch of the notes, or of the frequency of vibrations will be as follows:

'If we take do as 1 then re will be $9/8$, mi $5/4$, fa $4/3$, sol $3/2$, la $5/3$, si $15/8$, and do 2.

1	9/8	5/4	4/3	3/2	5/3	15/8	2
do	re	mi	fa	sol	la	si	do

'The differences in the acceleration or increase in the notes or the difference in tone will be as follows:

between do and re	$9/8$:	1	=	$9/8$	
between re and mi	$5/4$:	$9/8$	=	$10/9$	
between mi and fa	$4/3$:	$5/4$	=	$16/15$	increase retarded
between fa and sol	$3/2$:	$4/8$	=	$9/8$	
between sol and la	$5/3$:	$3/2$	=	$10/9$	
between la and si	$15/8$:	$5/3$	=	$9/8$	
between si and do	2 :	$15/8$	=	$16/15$	increase again retarded.'[6]

There are three kinds of intervals: 9/8, 10/9, 16/15. The two places where there is a retardation in the octave are the intervals *mi-fa* and *si-do* (16/15), where there is a semitone missing in the scale. 'In this respect when octaves are spoken of in a "cosmic" or a "mechanical" sense, only those intervals between *mi-fa* and *si-do* are called "*intervals*".'[7]

What happens in our own life? If we set ourselves some goal, it can be said that our action develops in accordance with the scheme of the octave. The octave of our action begins in the desired direction (Fig. 16.1).

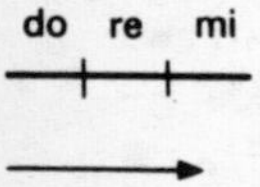

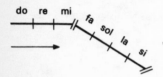

Figure 16.1

but at the first interval a deviation occurs (Fig. 16.2).

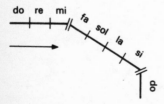

Figure 16.2

The same happens at the second interval (Fig. 16.3).

Figure 16.3

'The next octave gives an even more marked deviation, the one following that a deviation that is more marked still, so that the line of octaves may at last turn completely round' (Figs 16.4, 16.5).[8]
The line finally gives a complete ellipse (Fig. 16.5).

It is usually in this way that, once having defined particular goals which we consider it important to attain, instead of reaching them we are surprised to find ourselves deviating so far from our route that we do the opposite of what we want.

It is like this, says Gurdjieff, with everything that man under-

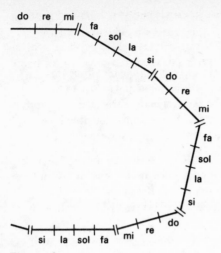

Figure 16.4

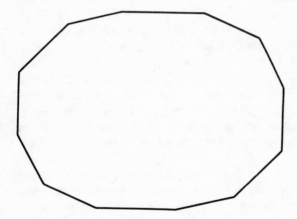

Figure 16.5

takes. What democracy does not eventually turn into tyranny, what faith does not breed intolerance, what disinterested search for truth does not culminate in the rigidity of a system?

It is worth pointing out that the word 'turn' is used as a synonym for 'deteriorate'. What is there in human relations that does not 'turn sour'? Even abundance may 'turn to excess'!

We are like weathercocks, and I wonder whether the ellipse shown above does not at some point open out into a spiral, that same spiral which for ever ornaments the 'august and tubiform belly' of Père Ubu, whose triumph over this century is evident enough.

Gurdjieff exclaims:

'Think how many turns the line of development of forces must have taken to come from the Gospel preaching of love to the Inquisition; or to go from the ascetics of the early centuries studying *esoteric* Christianity to the scholastics who calculated how many angels could be placed on the point of a needle.'[9]

Thus our powers deviate: from enthusiasm we almost inevitably turn to obstinacy, and we are consumed by the enormous monster unearthed by Baudelaire, whose name is Boredom.

We now come to the major cosmic octave, which is the ray of creation (Fig. 16.6).

The first note of the octave corresponds to the Absolute. As this is a descending scale, a shock is necessary between *do* and *si* in order for it to develop correctly. This shock is given by the very will of the Absolute. Then from *si* (all worlds) we go without difficulty to *la* (all suns), then to *sol* (sun) and *fa* (all planets). In other words it requires an 'additional shock' for the influences of the higher worlds to pass from *fa* (all planets) to *mi* (earth). Without this shock there would be a break between the earth and the other worlds. Gurdjieff states that this shock is provided by 'organic life on earth' and now the octave ends in *re* (the moon), then again *do*, which is *Nothing*. 'Between *All* and *Nothing* passes the ray of creation.'[10] Gurdjieff adds: 'Organic life represents so to speak the earth's organ of perception.'[11]

It can be said that there are 'human' octaves on the one hand and 'cosmic' octaves on the other. Normally the 'human' octaves are prolonged only by accident – which gives us the illusion that we are capable of *doing*, whereas in fact we are not able to achieve any of our goals on our own. On the other hand the 'cosmic' octaves develop unhindered, the 'shocks' coming when they are necessary in order to ensure their harmonious progression.

The 'man-machine' is the person who, because he sometimes manages to bring some project to completion, has the arrogance to think that he can do so in all circumstances, and claims an illusory freedom on behalf of himself and of all men.

Awakening begins at the moment when a man has become conscious of his weaknesses and limitations, when he observes that in

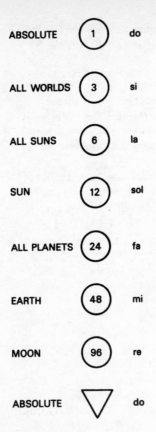

ABSOLUTE	1	do
ALL WORLDS	3	si
ALL SUNS	6	la
SUN	12	sol
ALL PLANETS	24	fa
EARTH	48	mi
MOON	96	re
ABSOLUTE	▽	do

Figure 16.6

most cases his actions elude his control, and that what he has the audacity to call his will is only a shapeless face humiliated day after day, and when he understands that unless he explores the cosmic mysteries – and these may be understood in prayer or meditation, or in a sudden intuitive grasp (illumination, *satori* or whatever) – man is nothing but a fragile toy in the heavy hands of nature. Rather than go on deluding himself, he decides to start humbly and without the least impatience to *listen*. This word is to be given the greatest possible content. I believe that the first quality to be cultivated with the utmost care is *attention*. There can be no doubt that when at last the unblinkered gaze is brought steadily to bear on the immeasurable that surrounds it, then, down the next street, in the corner of a bar, amid the buzz of the town or perhaps in the obscurity of a farmstead or a remote cottage that gaze will suddenly recognize the man who will reveal the truth.

What will this man say? Something rather like what Gurdjieff taught:

> 'The "man-machine" can do nothing. To him and around him everything *happens*. In order *to do* it is necessary to know the law of octaves, to know the moments of the "intervals" and be able to create necessary "additional shocks."
>
> 'It is only possible to learn this in a *school*, that is to say, in a rightly organized school which follows all esoteric traditions. Without the help of a school a man by himself can never understand the law of octaves, the points of the "intervals," and the order of creating "shocks." He cannot understand because certain conditions are necessary for this purpose, and these conditions can only be created in a school *which is itself created upon these principles*.'[12]

17 The lateral octave, the triple cosmic octave and the table of hydrogens

Inasmuch as man belongs to the world of living beings, like all living beings he plays the particular role assigned to him by nature, which is to enable higher influences to be transmitted to the earth. The very movement of life is sufficient for this purpose. Birth and death, agitation, even frenzy: all 'mechanical' actions, all outbursts of passion, all crimes, all wars, all sufferings release so many *vibrations* which together produce the shock needed to fill the interval *mi-fa*. These same vibrations also enable the moon, a 'planet in birth',[1] to grow, or rather evolve, to the point of becoming an earth in its turn.

So far the role of consciousness does not appear, and consciousness may even seem to be something superfluous. This is because man's destiny is twofold.

Man as man does not appear in the great octave of creation, but in a *lateral octave* stemming from the sun. In fact the 'intelligence of the sun' creates this new octave in order to fill the *mi-fa* interval of the major octave (Fig. 17.1).

Each note of the major octave may resonate as *do* at certain moments, engendering what we may call a lateral octave. In the same way, 'each note of any octave can be regarded as an octave on another plane' (Fig. 17.2).[2]

Three types of octave are distinguished in this way: the fundamental octaves, lateral octaves and inner octaves (although Gurdjieff states that the latter do not develop *ad infinitum*).

Returning to the lateral octave produced by the sun, the one in which man appears, we must first note that each of the 'worlds' that succeed each other along the fundamental cosmic octave possesses a dual nature. For example, the sun is certainly the celestial body we

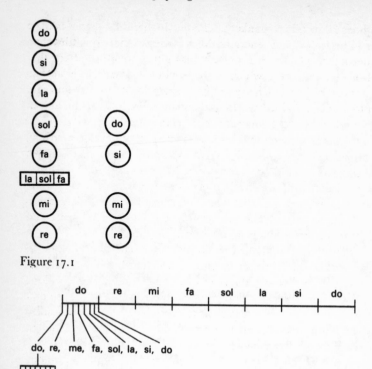

Figure 17.1

Figure 17.2

know, but like every planet or star it is also a living and above all an *intelligent* being. The sun's intelligence has two purposes in producing the lateral octave. First to create the 'sensitive film' which is organic life on earth. From this point of view man exists only for the needs of the octave, and man as an individual has no means of attaining higher forms of consciousness and life. But the sun also acts on its own behalf – it wants something. In creating man on earth it sets itself other objectives than simply filling an interval. It expects of man that he should progress from the level of the earth to its own level. Therefore it creates man, an *uncompleted* being. Man is certainly complete from the point of view of the fundamental octave. Like the animals and plants, he serves nature. But since he appears in the lateral octave and is endowed with consciousness, or rather he has the potential to develop consciousness within himself, from this other point of view we can say that he is an unfinished being, whose aptitudes allow him to hanker after a fate higher than that of being a mere diffuser of cosmic energies. Man possesses more qualities than are needed to play such a part; he has gifts enough to attain that level of mind or being which is the level of the sun. He is able to reach those worlds which are subject respectively to twenty-four and then to twelve laws, the world of the planets and of the sun, and in that world of the sun he may at last enjoy immortality.

Man cannot escape the law of accident, cannot develop anything but broken octaves in his life, except by submitting to the discipline of a school. This is the gist of Gurdjieff's unremitting advice to his own disciples, and which Ouspensky records in *In Search of the Miraculous*, although we must take care not to forget that there is also the way of the *obyvatel*, the 'way of life,' the way of good sense and uprightness which leads as far upward as the others.

But the schools mentioned by Gurdjieff are schools of the 'fourth way', one of whose forms are the groups which he himself assembled. In these schools, as I say, the work takes place simultaneously along the line of knowledge and along the line of being. We have seen that in the work major stress is laid on the acquisition of consciousness ('and all these things shall be added unto you'), and the student should not do anything whose necessity he does not understand.

In schools of the 'fourth way' a man exerts his efforts not in one direction but in three. It can be said that he works simultaneously on three octaves which are parallel, but whose original note does not sound at the same moment. These octaves do not develop independently, but on the contrary influence one another. The intervals of one octave are therefore filled thanks to the impulse of the other two.

The first octave represents *work for oneself*: self-study and study of the system are what we might call its two faces. This kind of work is egoistic, and that is necessary, but it comes from what Gurdjieff called 'conscious egoism'.

The second octave represents *work with and for others*. The pupil does not just take, he also gives – he must give, and give of himself, otherwise what he has taken palls, decays and finally annuls itself. And then there is so much which can only be understood at the moment where one is able to communicate it. Lastly, the inevitable clashes and tensions which occur among people play the part of 'shocks' and enable the pupil to progress.

The third octave represents *work for the school*. The foregoing efforts would be in vain if the pupil did not set ultimate goals beyond his immediate ends, and if he were not conscious of being entrusted, as far as his own resources permit, with a mission which goes far beyond any personal ambition.

Bearing in mind that Gurdjieff calls man a 'three-brained' being, a schematic view can be given in Fig. 17.3.

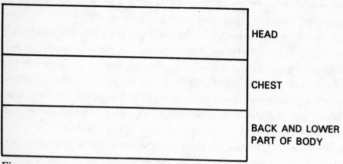

Figure 17.3

Inside this same diagram the (seven) centres are distributed as shown in Fig. 17.4.

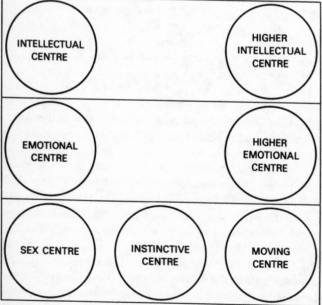

Figure 17.4

In ordinary life we are not even aware of the existence of the higher centres. It is not that they function wrongly, as happens with the other centres – on the contrary they are 'fully developed' in us. But because we do not supply them with the food they need, we are, so to speak, cut off from them.

This is because, not having learned how the 'human machine' works, we are bound to misuse it.

First we have to know what constitutes 'food for the machine'. Gurdjieff asserts that every living being feeds on what he calls 'hydrogens'. In order to understand what he means by this word we must picture the 'ray of creation' in a new form. To begin with, we shall confine ourselves only to the direct relationship of the Absolute to the sun, and then to the earth and the moon. We can show this relationship in Fig. 17.5.

Gurdjieff comments: 'It must be observed that although there are six "intervals" in these three octaves, only three of them actually require to be supplemented from outside.'[3] The others are filled by the will of the Absolute, by 'the influence of the sun's mass upon radiations passing through it', and by 'the action of the earth's mass upon radiations passing through it'.[4] As for the other intervals:

'We know nothing about the nature of the "shock" between *mi-fa* in the first octave Absolute-Sun. But the "shock" in the octave Sun-Earth is *organic life on earth*, that is, the three notes *la, sol, fa* of the octave which starts in the sun. The nature of the "shock" between *mi* and *fa* in the octave Earth-Moon is unknown to us.'[5]

We must now consider the octaves 'from the point of view of the law of three'. In the first, the note *do* 'conducts' the active force, which is designated by the number 1. The matter in which this force acts is 'carbon' (C).

Bear in mind that in Gurdjieff's cosmology everything is *matter*. Like other fundamental notions, this is a relative one. What we call 'matter' is only one of the aspects of what matter is in reality. All things, even the Absolute, can be defined in terms of the relation in them between 'matter' and 'vibrations'. 'The higher the "density of vibrations" the lower the "density of matter."'[6]

'The active force in the Absolute represents the maximum "density of vibrations," while the matter in which these vibrations proceed, that is, the first "carbon," represents the minimum density of matter.'[7]

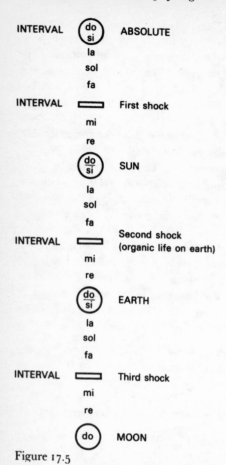

Figure 17.5

The note *si*, which is the conductor of the passive force (2), acts in its turn in 'oxygen', and the note *la*, through which the neutralizing force is transmitted, 'sounds' in 'nitrogen'.

Turning to the degree of activity of these forces, they appear in the order above – 'carbon', 'oxygen' and 'nitrogen' in the succession 1, 2, 3. But if we consider not their action but the matter in which they 'sound', they will be classified according to the density of this matter, that is in the order 1, 3, 2.

'"Carbon," "oxygen," and "nitrogen" together will give matter of the fourth order, or "hydrogen" (H), whose density we will designate by the number 6 (as the sum of 1, 2, 3), that is, H6.'[8]

So Gurdjieff defines the first triad in this way:

$$
\begin{array}{lccc}
do\ (C) & 1 & 1 & 1 \\
si\ (O) & 2 & 3 & 2 \\
la\ (N) & 3 & 2 & 3
\end{array} \Bigg\} H6
$$

The next triad is engendered from 'nitrogen', which is 'more active than "oxygen"', and which enters in this triad 'with the density of 2'.[9] The 'nitrogen' of each triad enters the next triad as 'carbon'.

So the second triad will be:

$$
\begin{array}{lccc}
la\ (C) & 2 & 2 & 2 \\
sol\ (O) & 4 & 6 & 4 \\
fa\ (N) & 6 & 4 & 6
\end{array} \Bigg\} H12
$$

The third:

$$
\begin{array}{lccc}
fa\ (C) & 4 & 4 & 4 \\
(shock) - (O) & 8 & 12 & 8 \\
mi\ (N) & 12 & 8 & 12
\end{array} \Bigg\} H24
$$

And so on, in accordance with the same principle, giving twelve triads whose last constitutes 'hydrogen' 12288 (Fig. 17.6).

Gurdjieff comments:

'Twelve "hydrogens" are obtained with densities ranging from 6 to 12288.

'These twelve "hydrogens" represent twelve categories of matter contained in the universe from the Absolute to the moon, and if it were possible to establish exactly which of these matters constitute man's organism and act in it, this alone would determine what place man occupies in the world.'[10]

'Irresolvable for us' are 'hydrogen' 6 and even 'hydrogen' 12. In order to be able to use the table of 'hydrogens' we have to reduce the table so that 'hydrogen' 12 becomes 'hydrogen' 1 (see Fig. 17.7).

All matters from 'hydrogen' 6 to 'hydrogen' 3072 are to be found and play a part in the human organism. In this table 'hydrogen' 768 is defined as *food*. To the category of 'hydrogens' 1536 and 3072 belong the inedible substances (for instance wood, or iron). 'Hydrogen' 384 designates water, 'hydrogen' 192 the air we breathe.

do	C	1	1	1	}							do	}
si	O	2	3	2	} H6							si	} H6
la	N	3	2	3	}	C	2	2	2	}		la	}
sol						O	4	6	4	} H12		sol	} H12
fa	C	4	4	4	}	N	6	4	6	}		fa	}
–	O	8	12	8	} H24							–	} H24
mi	N	12	8	12	}	C	8	8	8	}		mi	}
re						O	16	24	16	} H48		re	} H48
do	C	16	16	16	}	N	24	16	24	}		do	}
si	O	32	48	32	} H96							si	} H96
la	N	48	32	48	}	C	32	32	32	}		la	}
sol						O	64	96	64	} H192		sol	} H192
fa	C	64	64	64	}	N	96	64	96	}		fa	}
–	O	128	192	128	} H384							–	} H384
mi	N	192	128	192	}	C	128	128	128	}		mi	}
re						O	256	384	256	} H768		re	} H768
do	C	256	256	256	}	N	384	256	384	}		do	}
si	O	512	768	512	} H1536							si	} H1536
la	N	768	512	768	}	C	512	512	512	}		la	}
sol						O	1024	1536	1024	} H3072		sol	} H3072
fa	C	1024	1024	1024	}	N	1536	1024	1536	}		fa	}
–	O	2048	3072	2048	} H6144							–	} H6144
mi	N	3072	2048	3072	}	C	2048	2048	2048	}		mi	}
re						O	4096	6144	4096	} H12288		re	} H12288
do						N	6144	4096	6144	}		do	}

Figure 17.6

'"Hydrogen" 96 is represented by rarefied gases which man cannot breathe, but which play a very important part in his life; and further, this is the matter of animal magnetism, of emanations from the human body, of "n-rays," hormones, vitamins, and so on; in other words, with "hydrogen" 96 ends what is called matter or what is regarded as matter by our physics and chemistry. "Hydrogen" 96 also includes matters that are almost imperceptible to our chemistry or perceptible only by their traces or results, often merely presumed by some and denied by others.

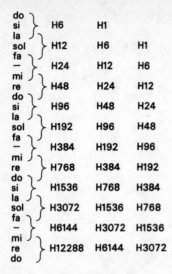

Figure 17.7 *Table of hydrogens*

'"Hydrogens" 48, 24, 12, and 6 are matters unknown to physics and chemistry, matters of our psychic and spiritual life on different levels.'[11]

18   Man considered as a 'three-story factory'

The missing element in man when he sets out to reform himself is *energy*. For he does not know how to produce it, nor how to conserve what little he has already been given by nature.

Man, who is so proud of his 'consciousness' and his 'powers', does not know what matter he is made of, what matters he should nourish himself on so as to allow his other 'bodies' to develop.

Food: he gives this word one meaning only, and the least important at that. And if he likes to think of himself as 'intelligent' he will affect to despise it – he will talk of 'feeding the brute' or 'putting the nosebag on', in the belief that his 'true self' is bound for higher things. He does not see that this 'self' which he honours so much that he would like to have it live in solitary state is only an emanation of the 'mechanical' part, either of his 'moving centre' or of his 'intellectual centre'.

In fact each centre is again divided into three parts, one 'intellectual', one 'emotional' and the third 'mechanical', which can be said to come to six parts, considering that each of them works sometimes positively and sometimes negatively. And in our life all that does not come from ourself and which derives from imitation, every thought which is not *our own thought*, is just a manifestation of the mechanical part of either the moving centre or, at best, the intellectual centre, when this is not totally asleep.

Anyone who wishes to *think for himself* and to *act* for himself, and who also wants his emotions to cease being 'negative', must learn not only how to accumulate energy but, moreover, how not to squander it. Gurdjieff explains:

'Energy is spent chiefly on unnecessary and unpleasant emotions, on the expectation of unpleasant things, possible and impossible, on bad moods, on unnecessary haste, nervousness, irritability, imagination, daydreaming, and so on. Energy is wasted on the wrong work of centers; on unnecessary tension of the muscles out of all proportion to the work produced; on perpetual chatter which absorbs an enormous amount of energy; on the "interest" continually taken in things happening around us or to other people and having in fact no interest whatever; on the constant waste of the force of "attention"; and so on, and so on.[1]

The struggle against these habits is necessary, but it is not sufficient. Let us picture man as a three-story factory (see Fig. 17.3). In everyday life this factory plays the part assigned to it by taking in and then transforming a certain number of substances. But the number of these substances is insufficient, and, furthermore, far from producing its full output the factory only operates a small number of the machines it houses. 'The factory actually produces nothing – all its machinery, all its elaborate equipment, actually serve no purpose at all, in that it maintains only with difficulty its own existence.'[2]

This is the way we are when we have allowed only our 'physical body' to grow.

But the factory's role should be to enable the other 'bodies' to grow, and this can only happen if it transforms a large number of 'coarse hydrogens' into 'finer hydrogens', if it becomes possible to 'save the fine "hydrogens"'.

It is a spiritual as well as a physical alchemy whose arcana Gurdjieff reveals:

'"Learn to separate the fine from the coarse" – this principle from the "Emerald Tablets of Hermes Trismegistus" refers to the work of the human factory, and if a man learns to "separate the fine from the coarse," that is, if he brings the production of the fine "hydrogens" to its possible maximum, he will by this very fact create for himself the possibility of an inner growth which can be brought about by no other means.'[3]

The development of the higher (astral and mental) bodies comes about, like that of the physical body, by means of the foods we absorb.

'The human organism receives three kinds of food:

1. The ordinary food we eat
2. The air we breathe
3. Our impressions.'[4]

Gurdjieff observes that whereas it is possible to go without food for a fairly long period it is not possible to go without air for more than two or three minutes without dying. But, 'without impressions a man cannot live a single moment.'[5]

In the three-story factory, physical food (H768) enters the lower story 'as "oxygen," *do* 768' (see Fig. 18.1).[6]

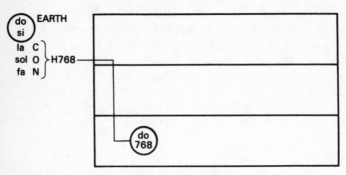

Figure 18.1 *'The entrance of food (H768) into the organism'*

In the organism, 'oxygen' 768 combines with 'carbon' 192 to produce 'nitrogen' N384. This 'nitrogen', the note *re* 384, becomes the 'oxygen' of the next triad, and meeting with 'carbon' 96 it produces a new 'nitrogen', N192, whose value in the octave will be *mi*.

Mi cannot pass into *fa* without a 'shock'. So the substance *mi* 192 cannot be transformed by itself. At the moment when *mi* sounds, entering the organism in the form of *do* 192, air brings the extra energy which enables it to pass into *fa*. *Fa* 96 unites with 'carbon' 24 and gives rise to 'nitrogen' 48. *Sol* 48 in turn, together with 'carbon' 12, produces 'nitrogen' 24. *La* 24 meets 'carbon' 6 and gives rise to 'nitrogen' 12.

'*Si* 12 is the highest substance produced in the organism from physical food with the help of the "additional shock" obtained from the air.'[7]

The 'food octave' is thus completed, thanks to the 'additional shock' from the air. The 'air octave' in its turn develops as and when in the organism the 'oxygens' meet the 'carbons' which are there.

The carbons are already present in the organism. They are designated by the sign:

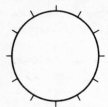

Thus air (*do* 192) enters the middle story of the factory as 'oxygen', to produce *re* 96 by uniting with 'carbon' 48. *Re* 96 meets 'carbon' 24 and now passes into *mi* 48.

The octave of air ends at this point, since no 'shock' intervenes to fill the interval *mi-fa*.

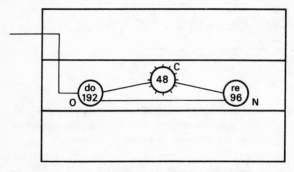

Figure 18.2   *'The beginning of the digestion of air in the organism'*

The 'octave of impressions' begins with *do* 48, which enters the top story of the factory as 'oxygen'.

Do 48 carries enough energy to pass into *re*, but 'the "carbon" 12 necessary for this is not present'.[8] 'At the same time *do* 48 does not come into contact with *mi* 48 so that it can neither itself pass into the next note nor give part of its energy to *mi* 48' (Fig. 18.3).[9]

This completes the *mechanical* development of the octaves. If the 'food octave' stops at *si* 12, the 'air octave' does not go beyond *mi* 48, and the 'octave of impressions' stops at the first note, *do* 48 (Fig. 18.4).

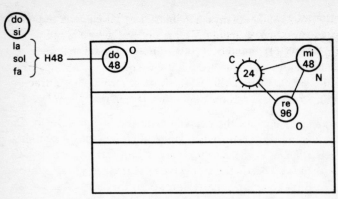

Figure 18.3 *'Entry of impressions into the organism'*

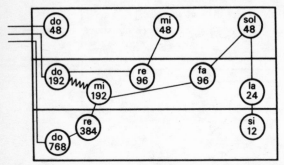

Figure 18.4 *'The three kinds of food and the digestion of H768 and H192 in the organism with the help of one mechanical "shock." The normal state of the organism and the normal production of finer substances from the products of nutrition'*

Yet is it possible to prolong both the 'air octave' and the 'octave of impressions'.

'For this purpose it is necessary to create a special kind of "artificial shock" at the point where the beginning of the third octave is arrested. This means that the "artificial shock" must be applied to the *note do 48.*'[10]

'Artificial shock': only 'self-remembering' can produce it. It is not enough to receive impressions passively:

'If I remember myself, I do not simply look at the street; I feel that I am looking, as though saying to myself: "I am looking." Instead of one impression of the street there are two impressions, one of the street and another of myself looking at it. This second impression, produced by the fact of my remembering myself, is the "additional shock." Moreover, it very often happens that the additional sensation connected with self-remembering brings with it an element of emotion, that is, the work of the machine attracts a certain amount of "carbon" 12 to the place in question.'[11]

So *consciousness* enables the octave of impressions to develop. *Do* 48, in passing into *re* 24, also acts upon *mi* 48, filling the interval that separates it from *fa*. While, on the octave of impressions, *do* 48 passes into *re* 24 then to *mi* 12, on the air octave *fa* 24 may pass to *sol* 12 then to *la* 6. '*La* 6 is the highest matter produced by the organism from air, that is, from the second kind of food.'[12]

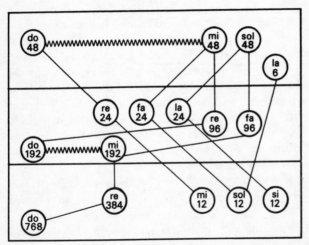

Figure 18.5 *'The complete picture of the intensive work of the organism and of the intensive production of substances from the products of nutrition after the first* conscious *"shock"'*

The man capable of 'self-remembering' and of producing the 'hydrogens' *si* 12 and *mi* 12 is that 'man number four' whose multiple 'I's are already unified. But the work does not stop there. A dual 'transmutation' must still occur, that of *si* 12 and especially of *mi* 12, which alone enable a new stage to be reached, and to come to the threshold where stands 'man number five'.

So once again the man has to create some 'volitional "shock"' to enable him to develop the octave of impressions. This is his only chance of making progress. But the nature of the second 'shock' is not clearly defined. I imagine that such a definition must be given in those groups where the work is going on under the guidance of an experienced teacher. However, this is what Gurdjieff said about it:

> 'The second volitional "shock" and transmutation become physically possible only after long practice on the first volitional "shock," which consists in self-remembering, and in observing the impressions received. On the way of the monk and on the way of the fakir work on the second "shock" begins before work on the first "shock," but as *mi* 12 is created only as a result of the first "shock," work, in the absence of other material, has of necessity to be concentrated on *si* 12, and it very often gives quite wrong results.'[13]

I think that we have to make a distinction here between 'conscious effort' and 'voluntary suffering', and it is unquestionably 'voluntary suffering' that plays the part of the second 'shock'. But if suffering, instead of being actively accepted, is simply undergone (and the ways of the monk and the fakir are ways of obedience), it concerns only the 'physical body', and having failed to induce the presence of 'hydrogen' *mi* 12 in his organism the man will expend his strength in vain, and will not reap the harvest of his abnegation. 'Right development on the fourth way must begin with the first volitional "shock" and then pass on to the second "shock" at *mi* 12.'[14]

We see that in ordinary life the slowest of the centres is the thinking or intellectual centre, which works with 'hydrogen' 48, whereas on the other hand the moving centre is fed by the 'many times quicker and more mobile' 'hydrogen' 24. As for the emotional centre, 'its work differs little in intensity and speed from the work of the moving center or the instinctive center.'[15]

From the moment when the 'additional shock' occurs, it is possible for a man to connect with the higher (emotional and intellectual) centres which work respectively with 'hydrogen' 12 and with 'hydrogen' 6.

So the work essentially consists in supervising the activity of all the centres, preventing any one of them from taking over the functions of another, but in particular allowing the higher centres to work. On these terms, man's name may finally cease to be *Legion*.

19 The enneagram

It was not my intention in the foregoing chapters to make an exhaustive study of Gurdjieff's cosmology. The task would be impossible. Instead I have set limits on myself, leaving out particular commentaries, insights or diagrams, not because I considered them unimportant but because it is not possible to include everything, and also because the interested reader will find them both in Ouspensky's *In Search of the Miraculous* and in Nicoll's *Psychological Commentaries*.

But it remains for me to speak of a diagram, the enneagram, through which Gurdjieff summed up, as it were, the whole of his teaching, or at any rate its cosmological aspects.

To understand this figure we must first look at the traditional symbols (Fig. 19.1).

Figure 19.1

Gurdjieff comments that these symbols,

'or the numbers 2, 3, 4, 5, 6, which express them, possess a definite meaning in relation to the inner development of man; they show different stages on the path of man's self-perfection and of the growth of his being.'[1]

The number 2, the parallel lines, symbolizes division, man 'taken as a *duality*'. The number 3, the triangle, reveals a new force, which is that of understanding. The number 4, the square, represents the man capable of action. The number 5, the pentagram, expresses the equilibrium of the man whose centres are functioning harmoniously. Finally the number 6, the six-pointed star, the Seal of Solomon, symbolizes the developed man.

The enneagram contains more meaning than all the preceding diagrams put together. It enables an understanding of man, as well as of all other realities, subject as they are to the Law of Three and to the Law of Seven.

The figure of the enneagram is shown in Fig. 19.2.

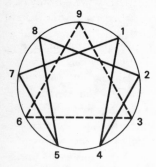

Figure 19.2

The circle is divided into nine equal segments, marking the transition from one octave to the next. The seven notes, the two intervals and the *do* of the next octave make a total of ten.

'In this way the law of octaves and the process of development it expresses, include the numbers 1 to 10. At this point we come to what may be termed the *symbolism of numbers*. The symbolism of numbers cannot be understood without the law of octaves or without a clear conception of how octaves are expressed in the *decimal system* and vice versa.'[2]

In studying this figure we notice that the second interval, which should come between *si* and *do*, appears out of sequence between *sol* and *la*. The normal figure would be as shown in Fig. 19.3.

'The apparent placing of the interval in *its wrong place* itself shows to those who are able to read the symbol what kind of "shock" is required for the passage of *si* to *do*.'[3]

How is the figure of the enneagram constructed? Any reality,

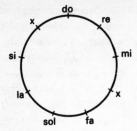

Figure 19.3

obeying the law of the octave, can be considered schematically as a whole (the circle) divisible into seven unequal parts. For the sake of convenience these parts are represented as equal. 'Taking a unit as one note containing within itself a whole octave,' it divides as follows:

1/7–0.142857
2/7–0.285714
3/7–0.428571
4/7–0.571428
5/7–0.714285
6/7–0.857142
7/7–0.999999

In each of the decimal numbers except the last, we find the same six digits. If we join the digits by straight lines in the order in which they appear in the first of these sequences, we obtain the enneagram inscribed in the circle, which symbolizes the law of seven.

The points 3, 6 and 9, which are not included in the preceding figure, form the equilateral triangle which symbolizes the Law of Three.

The enneagram may be understood in an infinite number of ways. I shall suggest only one of these, which will account for the fact that the interval falls between the notes *sol* and *la*, instead of between *si* and *do*.

Remember the three 'food octaves'. The first begins with the note *do* ('hydrogen' 768). This *do* passes into *re* ('hydrogen' 384), then to *mi* ('hydrogen' 192). At this point the second octave begins, its *do* filling the *mi-fa* interval of the first octave. On the enneagram this *do* is located at point number 3. *Do* 192 passes into *re* 96 then to *mi* 48. A new 'shock' is needed here, and it is the *do* of the 'octave of impressions' that produces it (when man, by 'self-remembering', redoubles its intensity). This *do* falls between the *sol* and *la* of the first octave, at point number 6. Now we see how the *sol-la* interval of the first octave, whose necessity had not been apparent, coincides with the *mi-fa* interval of the second octave, and is filled by the *do* of the third (see Fig. 19.4).

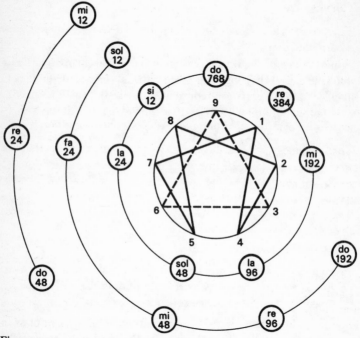

Figure 19.4

In fact it is not possible to study any reality without visualizing it in the context of a triple octave. An isolated octave only gives us a truncated image of things. This is one of the consequences, and an important one, of the Law of Three.

This is what Gurdjieff told Ouspensky when he explained to him how the word 'cosmos' is to be understood. First he showed him that there are seven cosmoses:

1 The Protocosmos, the 'first cosmos' – the Absolute.
2 The Ayocosmos, the 'holy cosmos' or 'Megalocosmos' – all worlds.

3 The Macrocosmos, the 'large cosmos' – all suns.

4 The Deuterocosmos, the 'second cosmos' – our sun.

5 The Mesocosmos, the 'middle cosmos' – all planets, or the earth, as representing the planetary world.

6 The Tritocosmos, the 'third cosmos' – man.

7 The Microcosmos, the 'small cosmos' – the atom.[4]

Then he said:

'Each cosmos is a living being which lives, breathes, thinks, feels, is born, and dies.

'All cosmoses result from the action of the same forces and the same laws. Laws are the same everywhere. But they manifest themselves in a different, or at least, in not quite the same way on different planes of the universe, that is, on different levels. Consequently cosmoses are not quite analogous one to another.'[5]

Gurdjieff added: 'It is only *three* cosmoses, taken together, that are similar and analogous to any other three.'[6] It is the same for the octaves: the 'food octaves' are analogous to the triple cosmic octave, and the enneagram enables us to understand either of them.

'Each completed whole,' Gurdjieff emphasized, 'each cosmos, each organism, *each plant*, is an enneagram.'[7]

The enneagram is seen as a universal symbol: 'All knowledge can be included in the enneagram and with the help of the enneagram it can be interpreted.'[8]

Lastly, the enneagram is also 'the same *perpetual motion* that men have sought since the remotest antiquity and could never find'. It is perpetual motion because the enneagram 'must be thought of as in motion, as moving'. 'It is *perpetual motion* and it is also the *philosopher's stone* of the alchemists.'[9]

In brief, the enneagram is in a sense the key which opens the gates of 'objective knowledge' to us and frees us from our prison of smug and fatal ignorance.

20   Remarkable men and remarkable sayings

There is the 'system', with its laws, its rules and its commandments, the garden laid out by the disciples in keeping with Gurdjieff's plans and tended by them with jealous care. But there is also life, a tangled forest whose mysteries and beauty cannot so easily be fathomed, unravelled and contemplated. For where the branches grow and intertwine the shadow is deep and the mouldering ground sometimes gives way. But where the road bends the sublime tree suddenly appears, and the heart is full. It seems to me that this is one of the lessons of *Meetings With Remarkable Men*.

That book will disappoint the intellectual, because of what is anecdotal and sometimes even trivial in it. Yet this commonplaceness is only on the surface. In the guise of telling stories, Gurdjieff teaches. Nor does he teach abstract precepts which together make up some sort of moral treatise; instead, on the occasion sometimes of everyday, sometimes of fantastic events, he shows us how we ought to behave, and points out the object of our pursuit.

The book appears as an exaltation of 'happy times'. In the Introduction Gurdjieff recalls the basic principles of his teaching, but in a figurative manner. He also formulates a biting critique of contemporary 'civilization' and its literature.

Gurdjieff contrasts 'word prostitution', whose aim is to pet the reader as you might pet a dog, with the sacred word of the Scriptures or the clear, refreshing word of traditional tales. Speaking of the *Thousand and One Nights*, he says: 'Anyone reading or hearing this book feels clearly that everything in it is fantasy, but fantasy corresponding to truth, even though composed of episodes which are quite improbable for the ordinary life of people.'[1]

The likelihood of the narrative, even its authenticity when it is autobiographical, remain secondary. The point is that the 'passing on of the torch' is done in unexpected ways, and that it is not enough to *say* what one means, one must also make it *understood* (in the 'being' sense of the word).

One therefore resorts to those 'skilful means' which I have already mentioned, and which include Gurdjieff's method of 'clouding the issue', shamelessly mingling the true with the false. As the translators of *Meetings With Remarkable Men* observe:

> For him the past is not worth recounting except in so far as it can serve as an example. In these tales of adventure what he suggests are not models for outward imitation, but a completely new way of facing life, which touches us directly and gives us a foretaste of another order of reality.[2]

It is up to us, and our own intuition, to sort out the real from the imaginary in this book, and up to us to pay attention to the various 'lessons' which it may contain.

In any case these lessons are simple. They speak not so much to our reason as to our heart, to the conscience hidden beneath the convolutions of habit and which it is the teacher's role to awaken by all possible means, no matter how painful.

We have too often repressed the promptings of our heart, for fear of seeming 'ridiculous'. That's childish, we say of things which we inwardly despise when we ought to hold them in the highest esteem. Childish, these precepts; childish, those rules? Haven't we all heard them before?

But Gurdjieff asks us: Who understands them? Who obeys them? Really, the teacher only teaches truisms. If the system may enable the intellectual to fulfil his destiny, the fact remains that his understanding of the system would be fruitless if unaccompanied by understanding of the *primal truths*.

On some of these, Gurdjieff was implacable. For example, and perhaps above all, he was insistent on the fact that knowledge is empty when it is not accompanied by a parallel development of being. Remember the hackneyed saying of Rabelais, so often analysed yet so rarely understood, that 'science without conscience is only the ruin of the soul'. In order not to ruin that soul, what we must do is precisely to keep it, or make it, childish. 'Verily I say unto you, Except ye be converted, and become as little children, ye shall not enter into the kingdom of heaven.'[3]

It is as children that we must read *Meetings With Remarkable Men* – as children capable of wonder, of following where the storyteller leads, and also of identifying with the marvellous living figures whom we see. Anybody who came to this book in search of *new* revelations, or *new* methods of achieving the consciousness without which it remains useless to utter the word freedom, would be quickly disenchanted.

Gurdjieff, like his father, is an *ashokh*, 'the name given everywhere in Asia and the Balkan peninsula to the local bards, who composed, recited or sang poems, songs, legends, folk-tales, and all sorts of stories.'[4]

Rather than being *read*, he has to be heard.

The other basic lesson of the book is that we are alive. It is in life, in what is around us, that we should look for the truth, for the signs of God's presence. Given that we keep our eyes open, it is also in life that we meet those remarkable men described by Gurdjieff. Certainly in the West the bustle of busy towns muddles and confuses everything, and things are not so straightforward, drawn as we are by false promises, incapable as we too often are of recognizing authenticity. All this requires both discrimination and naivety together.

At the time he writes this book, Gurdjieff is already an ageing man, not bitter, but weary of knocking on the armoured door of human foolishness, and determined not to speak in any standard language but in a new language (undoubtedly a very ancient language whose flavour has been forgotten).

He evokes sublime moments of the past, but also hours of weakness or doubt, without indulgence.

To conclude this book I have chosen three extracts from *Meetings With Remarkable Men*, the first recalling Gurdjieff's father, the second his first tutor, Father Borsh, and the third Father Giovanni, whose words may provide us with a final lesson.[5]

1

The individuality and intellectuality of my father can, in my opinion, be very well pictured in the mind's eye of the reader if I quote here a few of his many favourite 'subjective sayings', which he often used in conversation.

In this connection, it is interesting to remark that I, as well as many others, noticed that when he himself used these sayings in conversation, it always seemed to every hearer that they could not have been more apt or better put, but that if anyone else made use of them, they seemed to be entirely beside the point or improbable nonsense.

Some of these subjective sayings of his were as follows:

Without salt, no sugar.
Ashes come from burning.
The cassock is to hide a fool.
He is deep down, because you are high up.
If the priest goes to the right, then the teacher must without fail turn to the left.
If a man is a coward, it proves he has will.
A man is satisfied not by the quantity of food, but by the absence of greed.
Truth is that from which conscience can be at peace.
No elephant and no horse – even the donkey is mighty.
In the dark a louse is worse than a tiger.
If there is 'I' in one's presence, the God and Devil are of no account.
Once you can shoulder it, it's the lightest thing in the world.
A representation of Hell – a stylish shoe.
Unhappiness on earth is from the wiseacring of women.
He is stupid who is 'clever'.
Happy is he who sees not his unhappiness.
The teacher is the enlightener; who then is the ass?
Fire heats water, but water puts out fire.
Genghis Khan was great, but our policeman, so please you, is still greater.
If you are first, your wife is second; if your wife is first, you had better be zero: only then will your hens be safe.
If you wish to be rich, make friends with the police.
If you wish to be famous, make friends with the reporters.
If you wish to be full – with your mother-in-law.
If you wish to have peace – with your neighbour.
If you wish to sleep – with your wife.
If you wish to lose your faith – with the priest.

To give a fuller picture of my father's individuality, I must say something about a tendency of his nature rarely observed in contemporary people, and striking to all who knew him well. It was chiefly on account of this tendency that from the very beginning, when he became poor and had to go into business, his affairs went so badly that his friends and those who had business dealings with him considered him unpractical and even not clever in this domain.

And indeed, every business that my father carried on for the purpose of making money always went wrong and brought none of the results obtained by others. However, this was not because he was unpractical or lacked mental ability in this field, but only because of this tendency.

This tendency of his nature, apparently acquired by him when still a child, I would define thus: 'an instinctive aversion to deriving personal advantage for himself from the naïveté and bad luck of others'.

In other words, being highly honourable and honest, my father could never consciously build his own welfare on the misfortune of his neighbour. But most of those round him, being typical contemporary people, took advantage of his honesty and deliberately tried to cheat him, thus unconsciously belittling the significance of that trait in his psyche which conditions the whole of Our Common Father's commandments for man.

Indeed, there could be ideally applied to my father the following paraphrase of a sentence from sacred writings, which is quoted at the present time by the followers of all religions everywhere, for describing the abnormalities of our daily life and for giving practical advice:

Strike – and you will not be struck.
But if you do not strike – they will beat you to death, like Sidor's goat.

In spite of the fact that he often happened to find himself in the midst of events beyond the control of man and resulting in all sorts of human calamities, and in spite of almost always encountering dirty manifestations from the people round him – manifestations recalling those of jackals – he did not lose heart, never identified himself with anything, and remained inwardly free and always himself.

The absence in his external life of everything that those round him regarded as advantages did not disturb him inwardly in the least; he was ready to reconcile himself to anything, provided there were only bread and quiet during his established hours for meditation.

What most displeased him was to be disturbed in the evening when he would sit in the open looking at the stars.

I, for my part, can only say now that with my whole being I would desire to be able to be such as I knew him to be in his old age.

Owing to circumstances of my life not dependent on me, I have not personally seen the grave where the body of my dear father lies, and it is unlikely that I will ever be able, in the future, to visit his grave. I therefore, in concluding this chapter devoted to my father, bid any of my sons, whether by blood or in spirit, to seek out, when he has the possibility, this solitary grave, abandoned by force of circumstances ensuing chiefly from that human scourge called the herd instinct, and there to set up a stone with the inscription:

> I AM THOU,
> THOU ART I,
> HE IS OURS,
> WE BOTH ARE HIS.
> SO MAY ALL BE
> FOR OUR NEIGHBOUR.

2

Father Borsh had a very original idea of the world and of man.

His views on man and the aim of man's existence differed completely from those of the people round him and from everything I had heard or gathered from my reading.

I will mention here certain thoughts of his which may serve to illustrate the understanding he had of man and what he expected of him.

He said:

'Until adulthood, man is not responsible for any of his acts, good or bad, voluntary or involuntary; solely responsible are the people close to him who have undertaken, consciously or owing to accidental circumstances, the obligation of preparing him for responsible life.

'The years of youth are for every human being, whether male or female, the period given for the further development of the initial conception in the mother's womb up to, so to say, its full completion.

'From this time on, that is, from the moment the process of his development is finished, a man becomes personally responsible for all his voluntary and involuntary manifestations.

'According to laws of nature elucidated and verified through many centuries of observation by people of pure reason, this process of development is finished in males between the ages of twenty and twenty-three, and in females between the ages of fifteen and nineteen, depending on the geographical conditions of the place of their arising and formation.

'As elucidated by wise men of past epochs, these age periods have been established by nature, according to law, for the acquisition of independent being with personal responsibility for all one's manifestations, but unfortunately at the present time they are hardly recognized at all. And this, in my opinion, is owing chiefly to the negligent attitude in contemporary education towards the question of sex, a question which plays the most important role in the life of everyone.

'As regards responsibility for their acts, most contemporary people who have reached or even somewhat passed the age of adulthood, strange as it may seem at first glance, may prove to be not responsible for any of their manifestations; and this, in my opinion, can be considered conforming to law.

'One of the chief causes of this absurdity is that, at this age, contemporary people in most cases lack the corresponding type of the opposite sex necessary, according to law, for the completion of their type, which, from causes not dependent upon them but ensuing, so to say, from Great Laws, is in itself a "something not complete".

'At this age, a person who does not have near him a corresponding type of the opposite sex for the completion of his incomplete type, is nonetheless subject to the laws of nature and so cannot remain without gratification of his sexual needs. Coming in contact with a type not corresponding to his own and, owing to the law of polarity, falling in certain respects under the influence of this non-corresponding type, he loses, involuntarily and imperceptibly, almost all the typical manifestations of his individuality.

'That is why it is absolutely necessary for every person, in the process of his responsible life, to have beside him a person of the opposite sex of corresponding type for mutual completion in every respect.

'This imperative necessity was, among other things, providentially well understood by our remote ancestors in almost all past epochs and, in order to create conditions for a more or less normal collective existence, they considered it their chief task to be able to make as well and as exactly as possible the choice of types from opposite sexes.

'Most of the ancient peoples even had the custom of making these choices between the two sexes, or betrothals, in the boy's seventh year with a girl one year old. From this time on the two families of the future couple, thus early betrothed, were under the mutual obligation of assisting the correspondence in both children of all the habits inculcated in the course of growth, such as inclinations, enthusiasms, tastes and so on.'

I also very well remember that on another occasion the father dean said:

'In order that at responsible age a man may be a real man and not a parasite, his education must without fail be based on the following ten principles.

'From early childhood there should be instilled in the child:

Belief in receiving punishment for disobedience.
Hope of receiving reward only for merit.
Love of God – but indifference to the saints.
Remorse of conscience for the ill-treatment of animals.
Fear of grieving parents and teachers.
Fearlessness towards devils, snakes and mice.
Joy in being content merely with what one has.
Sorrow at the loss of the goodwill of others.
Patient endurance of pain and hunger.
The striving early to earn one's bread.'

To my great distress, I did not happen to be present during the last days of this worthy and, for our time, remarkable man, in order to pay the last debt of earthly life to him, my unforgettable tutor, my second father.

One Sunday, many years after his death, the priests and congregation of the Kars Military Cathedral were much astonished and interested when a man quite unknown in the neighbourhood requested the full funeral service to be held over a lonely and forgotten grave, the only one within the grounds of the cathedral.

And they saw how this stranger with difficulty held back his tears and, having generously recompensed the priests and without looking at anyone, told the coachman to drive to the station.

Rest in peace, dear Teacher! I do not know whether I have justified or am justifying your dreams, but the commandments you gave me I have never once in all my life broken.

3

'Faith cannot be given to man. Faith arises in a man and increases in its action in him not as the result of automatic learning, that is, not from any automatic ascertainment of height, breadth, thickness, form and weight, or from the perception of anything by sight, hearing, touch, smell or taste, but from understanding.

'Understanding is the essence obtained from information intentionally learned and from all kinds of experiences personally experienced.

'For example, if my own beloved brother were to come to me here at this moment and urgently entreat me to give him merely a tenth part of my understanding, and if I myself wished with my whole being to do so, yet I could not, in spite of my most ardent desire, give him even the thousandth part of this understanding, as he has neither the knowledge nor the experience which I have quite accidentally acquired and lived through in my life.

'No, Professor, it is a hundred times easier, as it is said in the Gospels, "for a camel to pass through the eye of a needle" than for anyone to give to another the understanding formed in him about anything whatsoever.

'I formerly also thought as you do and even chose the activity of a missionary in order to teach everyone faith in Christ. I wanted to make everyone as happy as I myself felt from faith in the teachings of Jesus Christ. But to wish to do that by, so to say, grafting faith on by words is just like wishing to fill someone with bread merely by looking at him.

'Understanding is acquired, as I have already said, from the totality of information intentionally learned and from personal experiencings; whereas knowledge is only the automatic remembrance of words in a certain sequence.

'Not only is it impossible, even with all one's desire, to give to another one's own inner understanding, formed in the course of

life from the said factors, but also, as I recently established with
certain other brothers of our monastery, there exists a law that the
quality of what is perceived by anyone when another person tells
him something, either for his knowledge or his understanding,
depends on the quality of the data formed in the person speaking.

'To help you understand what I have just said, I will cite as
an example the fact which aroused in us the desire to make investigations and led us to the discovery of this law.

'I must tell you that in our brotherhood there are two very old
brethren; one is called Brother Ahl and the other Brother Sez.
These brethren have voluntarily undertaken the obligation of
periodically visiting all the monasteries of our order and
explaining various aspects of the essence of divinity.

'Our brotherhood has four monasteries, one of them ours, the
second in the valley of the Pamir, the third in Tibet, and the
fourth in India. And so these brethren, Ahl and Sez, constantly
travel from one monastery to another and preach there.

'They come to us once or twice a year. Their arrival at our
monastery is considered among us a very great event. On the days
when either of them is here, the soul of every one of us experiences
pure heavenly pleasure and tenderness.

'The sermons of these two brethren, who are to an almost equal
degree holy men and who speak the same truths, have nevertheless a different effect on all our brethren and on me in particular.

'When Brother Sez speaks, it is indeed like the song of the birds
in Paradise; from what he says one is quite, so to say, turned
inside out; one becomes as though entranced. His speech "purls"
like a stream and one no longer wishes anything else in life but to
listen to the voice of Brother Sez.

'But Brother Ahl's speech has almost the opposite effect. He
speaks badly and indistinctly, evidently because of his age. No one
knows how old he is. Brother Sez is also very old – it is said three
hundred years old – but he is still a hale old man, whereas in
Brother Ahl the weakness of old age is clearly evident.

'The stronger the impression made at the moment by the words
of Brother Sez, the more this impression evaporates, until there
ultimately remains in the hearer nothing at all.

'But in the case of Brother Ahl, although at first what he says
makes almost no impression, later, the gist of it takes on a definite

form, more and more each day, and is instilled as a whole into the heart and remains there for ever.

'When we became aware of this and began trying to discover why it was so, we came to the unanimous conclusion that the sermons of Brother Sez proceeded only from his mind, and therefore acted on our minds, whereas those of Brother Ahl proceeded from his being and acted on our being.

'Yes, Professor, knowledge and understanding are quite different. Only understanding can lead to being, whereas knowledge is but a passing presence in it. New knowledge displaces the old and the result is, as it were, a pouring from the empty into the void.

'One must strive to understand; this alone can lead to our Lord God.

'And in order to be able to understand the phenomena of nature, according and not according to law, proceeding around us, one must first of all consciously perceive and assimilate a mass of information concerning objective truth and the real events which took place on earth in the past; and secondly, one must bear in oneself all the results of all kinds of voluntary and involuntary experiencings.'

Biographical note

George Ivanovitch Gurdjieff was born on 13 January 1877 in the town of Alexandropol, not far from the citadel of Kars, which had just fallen into Russian hands.

His family was of Greek origin. After escaping from Byzantium and from Turkish persecution, his ancestors had settled on the eastern shores of the Black Sea, and then in Georgia.

His father 'was widely known . . . as an *ashokh*, that is, a poet and narrator'.[1] The *ashokhs* were local bards who

> not only knew by heart innumerable and often very lengthy
> narratives and poems, and sang from memory all their various
> melodies, but when improvising in their own, so to say, subjective
> way, they hit upon the appropriate rhymes and changes of rhythm
> for their verses with astounding rapidity.[2]

Gurdjieff declared that the stories his father would tell 'on the evenings before Sundays and holidays' had 'left their mark on my whole life'.[3]

Gurdjieff's father had been a wealthy man. He had owned big cattle herds, and followed the custom of looking after cattle belonging to 'the poorer families' in the region. Gurdjieff writes: 'But just when his herd had been increased in this way by several thousand head of other people's cattle, a cattle plague came from Asia and spread all over Transcaucasia.'[4]

Herds were decimated. Gurdjieff's father was ruined, and now that he was poor he took up the craft of carpentry.

After attending the Greek school in Kars for a while, Gurdjieff entered the Russian municipal school, where he displayed his extreme precocity:

As I was very quick at my studies, I wasted very little time on the preparation of lessons, and in all my spare time I helped my father in his workshop. Very soon I even began to have my own circle of customers, first among my comrades, for whom I made various things such as guns, pencil-boxes and so on; and later, little by little, I passed on to more serious work, doing all kinds of small repairs in people's houses.[5]

Gurdjieff always kept up his talent for earning his living by the most seemingly pedestrian methods. This was often brought up against him, but he took a sarcastic pride in defending himself in the superb essay 'The Material Question', which is printed as an appendix to *Meetings With Remarkable Men*.

From the time he entered the Russian school, where he studied under the direction of Dean Borsh, the man he was to call 'the third aspect of my inner God', Gurdjieff asked himself a lot of questions which were not answered in school books. Later he wrote:

This original personality of mine, already 'smelled out' by certain definite individuals from both choirs of the Judgment Seat Above, whence Objective justice proceeds, and also here on Earth, by as yet a very limited number of people, is based . . . on three secondary specific data formed in me at different times during my preparatory age.'[6]

This is how Gurdjieff defines the first of these 'data':

in my entirety a 'something' arose which in respect of any kind of so to say 'aping,' that is to say, imitating the ordinary automatized manifestations of those around me, always and in everything engendered what I should now call an 'irresistible urge' to do things not as others do them.'[7]

Not only did Gurdjieff obey that urge throughout his life, but he also strove to kindle it in the 'general presence' of his contemporaries. Many people held this against him, imagining, out of who knows what idealized version of the man of God, that it is enough to imitate in order to achieve wisdom or holiness.

The second 'datum' crystallized some time later in the form of

a tendency to seek out the causes of the arising of every suspicious 'actual fact'; and this property . . . gradually and automatically led to my ultimately becoming a specialist in the investigation of every suspicious phenomenon which, as it so often happened, came my way.[8]

The third 'datum' manifested itself in the form of an 'all-universal principle of living' which Gurdjieff never ceased to practise and which he formulated as follows:

'If you go on a spree then go the whole hog including the postage.'[9]

So Gurdjieff refused the fine future in store for him as a priest or doctor, and his extreme curiosity took him travelling all over the East, as far as Tibet.

What he was looking for were traces of the 'old knowledge' which survived here and there, he felt sure, in ruined temples, in monasteries and in ancient storage chests.

The reader can refer to Gurdjieff's autobiography for details of these travels, and of his meeting with the group of Seekers of Truth. In fact all we know about the life he led for twenty years is what he himself chose to reveal.

> But if [*Meetings With Remarkable Men*] is an autobiography it is certainly not an autobiography in the ordinary sense of the word. [The reader] should not take everything literally, but nor should he turn everything into symbols either, or try to work back to the sources of the author's knowledge by attempting any systematic exploration of the course of the River Pyandzh or the mountains of Kafiristan. For although the narrative has a ring of undeniable authenticity, it seems obvious that Gurdjieff meant to cover his tracks.[10]

In 1913 Gurdjieff was back in Russia. It was in the spring of 1915, in a Moscow café, that his meeting with Ouspensky occurred. Ouspensky, already the author of *Tertium Organum*, had just returned from travels in India and the East 'to look for a *school* or *schools*'.[11]

Ouspensky describes how

> I saw a man of an oriental type, no longer young, with a black mustache and piercing eyes, who astonished me first of all because he seemed to be disguised and completely out of keeping with the place and its atmosphere. I was still full of impressions of the East. And this man with the face of an Indian raja or an Arab sheik whom I at once seemed to see in a white burnoose or a gilded turban, seated here in this little café, where small dealers and

commission agents met together, in a black overcoat with a velvet collar and a black bowler hat, produced the strange, unexpected, and almost alarming impression of a man poorly disguised.[12]

But that first impression quickly faded, to give way to fascination: 'Not only did my questions not embarrass him but it seemed to me that he put much more into each answer than I had asked for. I liked his manner of speaking, which was careful and precise.'[13]

From that day on, Ouspensky became Gurdjieff's pupil. It is to him that we owe that rigorous account of Gurdjieff's words, and of the work which was done in the groups he formed, *In Search of the Miraculous*, or 'Fragments of an Unknown Teaching', as it is subtitled.

In 1916, in St Petersburg, the composer Thomas de Hartmann heard about Gurdjieff and his work and asked to meet him. Gurdjieff arranged to meet him at 'Palkin's' – 'Palkin's', de Hartmann recalls 'is the name of a huge restaurant on the corner of Nevsky Prospekt, the main street in St Petersburg, but a guards officer [de Hartmann had just been called up as a reserve officer] would never dare to frequent it.'[14]

Recalling that first meeting, de Hartmann writes:

> The atmosphere had certainly been planned by Gurdjieff himself, from Palkin's restaurant to the café where at one point he had said:
> 'Usually there are more whores here.'
> Everything, including that coarse observation, was supposed to repel the newcomer, or at least to compel him to overcome his aversions, to stand fast and persevere in spite of everything.[15]

Next year Gurdjieff assembled a number of his disciples in the town of Essentuki, in the northern Caucasus. There he set out to found an 'Institute for the Harmonious Development of Man'.

His pupils were subjected to very hard exercises whose necessity they did not initially understand, but which were to enable part of the group to undertake a hard and even perilous journey at the moment when civil war was breaking out, and enable Gurdjieff to lead his flock safely to Tiflis, then to Constantinople, and a little later to Germany and then to France, where he settled in 1922. In each of the towns where he stayed Gurdjieff established the basis of an Institute, but it was only at the 'Prieuré' of Avon, in the property made over to him by the widow of Maître Labori, Dreyfus's lawyer, that he was finally able to unite his community around him in a lasting way.

Most of his new pupils, and even inquisitive visitors, were sent to him by Ouspensky, who had settled in London after parting with his teacher.

Among Gurdjieff's English disciples, a few figures are outstanding. Orage, the discerning man of letters, founder of the review the *New Age*, which he sold to come to the Prieuré. C. S. Nott, author of two volumes of memoirs, *Teachings of Gurdjieff* and *Further Teachings of Gurdjieff*, invaluable accounts by an honourable and intelligent man. Margaret Anderson, whose book *The Unknowable Gurdjieff* is essential reading:

> in New York in 1914 she had founded an avant-garde magazine,
> *The Little Review*, in which America had been introduced to
> Apollinaire, Cocteau, Gide, Satie, Schoenberg, Picasso,
> Modigliani and Braque. . . . She had even risked imprisonment
> for venturing to publish Joyce's *Ulysses* there.[16]

Finally Katherine Mansfield, who came to the Prieuré in the terminal phase of consumption, and died there – for which Gurdjieff, who had only accepted her on the insistence of Orage and his friends, 'received the due amount of lies and slanders', as Ouspensky wrote.[17]

Even children lived at the Prieuré. The American Fritz Peters has left an account of the childhood years he spent close to Gurdjieff under the title of *Boyhood With Gurdjieff*. He also wrote a book of reminiscences called *Gurdjieff Remembered*.

It can be said that Gurdjieff's 'public life' really begins with the foundation of the Prieuré. In 1923 his pupils gave a display of sacred dances and 'movements' at the Théâtre des Champs Elysées in Paris. Gurdjieff always attached tremendous importance to anything to do with the body, to the point of signing *Beelzebub's Tales to His Grandson* as follows:

> He who in childhood was called 'Tatakh'; in early youth 'Darky';
> later the 'Black Greek'; in middle age, the 'Tiger of Turkestan';
> and now, not just anybody, but the genuine 'Monsieur' or
> 'Mister' Gurdjieff, or the nephew of 'Prince Mukransky,' or
> finally, simply a 'Teacher of Dancing.'[18]

Other artists and intellectuals followed the teaching of Gurdjieff. Mention must be made of Alexandre de Salzmann, the painter and theatrical designer, whose wife 'was subsequently to make Gurdjieff's thought known in France, and to bring him the groups to which he passed on his teaching in Paris after the closure of the Prieuré'.[19]

It was through Alexandre de Salzmann that René Daumal became acquainted with that teaching. His *Mount Analogue* 'is a quite transparent transposition of the inner experience that Daumal and his companions pursued'.[20] *A Night of Serious Drinking*, Daumal's other and older 'novel', appears, like the *Tales*, as 'an objectively impartial criticism of the life of man'.

In 1924 Gurdjieff went to New York with his pupils to give further performances of his 'movements'.

A few weeks after his return he was injured in a car accident on the road from Paris to Fontainebleau. Gurdjieff was badly hurt, but thanks to his rare vitality he recovered and took advantage of his convalescence to write the first of his books, *Beelzebub's Tales to His Grandson*. At the same time he partially closed down the Institute.

He now devoted the best part of his energies to the craft of writing, applying himself to it 'with the same craftsman's aptitude which had enabled him in his youth to learn so many other crafts'.[21]

This is how he described his situation at the end of *Beelzebub's Tales*:

After six years of work, merciless toward myself and with almost continuously tense mentation, I yesterday at last completed the setting down on paper, in a form, I think, accessible to everybody, the first of the three series of books I had previously thought out and six years ago begun – just those three series in which I planned to actualize by means of the totality of the ideas to be developed, at first in theory and afterwards in practice, also by a means I had foreseen and prepared, three essential tasks I had set myself: namely, by means of the first series, to destroy in people everything which, in their false representations, as it were, exists in reality, or in other words 'to corrode without mercy all the rubbish accumulated during the ages in human mentation'; by means of the second series, to prepare so to say 'new constructional material'; and by means of the third, 'to build a new world.'[22]

Gurdjieff's second work is entitled *Meetings With Remarkable Men*. The third, which has not been published, is entitled *Life Is Real Only Then, When 'I Am'*.

Meanwhile Gurdjieff 'never stopped composing music; nearly every day, on a kind of portable harmonium, he improvised hymns, prayers or melodies of Kurdish, Armenian or Afghan origin, which Thomas de Hartmann took down and transcribed.'[23]

When he had completed his work he sold the Prieuré of Avon. The decision to abandon the Institute had been taken for some time:

I was constrained with an inexpressible impulse of grief and despondency to make this decision to liquidate this institution and everything organized and carefully prepared for the opening the following year of eighteen sections in different countries, in short, of everything I had previously created with almost superhuman labor, chiefly because, soon after the said accident occurred, that is, three months afterwards, when the former usual functioning of my mentation had been more or less reestablished in me – I being still utterly powerless in body – I then reflected that the attempt to preserve the existence of this institution, would in the absence of real people around me and owing to the impossibility of procuring without me the great material means required for it, inevitably lead to a castastrophe the result of which, among other things for me in my old age as well as for numerous others wholly dependent on me, would be, so to say, a 'vegetation.'[24]

From 1933 onward, Gurdjieff lived in Paris. While the Institute no longer existed in its old form, Gurdjieff had numerous pupils around him, and there were groups created under his indirect guidance. Until 1939 he paid frequent visits to the United States, where new pupils awaited him.

During the war he seldom left his flat in the Rue des Colonels-Renard, except for example to take an orange to the dying Luc Dietrich. This has been seen as a paltry gesture. I know of nothing that moves me more.

Gurdjieff died in Paris on 29 October 1949. Since then, the groups he formed have continued their activities, in silence and in secret.

Notes

The three volumes of *Beelzebub's Tales to His Grandson* (abbreviated in these Notes to BT I, II and III) and *Meetings With Remarkable Men* (abbreviated to MWRM) are published in 'authorized' versions which I have quoted verbatim. The publisher's note to *Beelzebub's Tales* reads:

> Original written in Russian and Armenian. Translations into other languages have been made under the personal direction of the author by a group of translators chosen by him and specially trained according to their defined individualities, in conformity with the text to be translated and in relation to the philological particularities of each language.

The publisher's note to the Routledge edition of *Meetings With Remarkable Men* (1977) reads:

> Written in Russian, the manuscript of this book was begun in 1927 and revised by the author over a period of many years. The first English translation by A. R. Orage has been revised and reworked from the Russian for this publication.

> P. D. Ouspensky's record of his eight years of work as Gurdjieff's pupil, *In Search of the Miraculous*, was originally published in English. The title is abbreviated in the Notes to ISM. (Tr.)

1   Reflections on the 'inhumanity' of Gurdjieff

1 ISM. p. 102.
2 Matthew 5: 29

3 BT I, p. 23.
4 ISM, p. 362.
5 Idries Shah, *The Sufis*, London, Jonathan Cape, 1969, p. 68.
6 Matthew 10: 34.
7 Matthew 7: 6.

2 The 'way of blame'

1 In French:

> La sottise, l'erreur, le péché, la lésine,
> Occupent nos esprits et travaillent nos corps
> Et nous alimentons nos aimables remords
> Comme les mendiants nourrissent leur vermine.
>
> Nos péchés sont têtus, nos repentirs sont lâches;
> Nous nous faisons payer grassement nos aveux,
> Et nous rentrons gaiement dans le chemin bourbeux,
> Croyant par de vils pleurs laver toutes nos taches.

The English translation is taken from Joanna Richardson's selection, *Baudelaire*, London, Penguin Books, 1975, p. 27.

2 *Lautréamont's Maldoror*, translated by Alexis Lykiard, London, Allison & Busby, 1970, p. 3.
3 Letter to Paul Démeny, 15 May 1871, translated from Rimbaud, *Oeuvres complètes*, Paris, Bibliothèque de la Pléiade, 1914.
4 Translated from 'Mon coeur mis à nu', LXXXI, Baudelaire, *Oeuvres complètes*, Paris, Bibliothèque de la Pléiade, 1961.
5 BT I, p. 107.
6 ISM, pp. 159–60.
7 Translated from André Breton, *Anthologie de l'humour noir*, Paris, J.-J. Pauvert, 1966, p. 9 f.
8 D. T. Suzuki, *Essays in Zen Buddhism: Third Series*, London, Rider & Co., 1958, p. 59.
9 Breton, op. cit., p. 10.
10 Baudelaire, 'De l'Essence du rire', *Oeuvres complètes*, op. cit., pp. 710 f.
11 ISM, p. 159.
12 Henri Tracol, *Georges Ivanovitch Gurdjieff, l'éveil et la pratique du 'rappel de soi'*, publisher unnamed, p. 9. Translated as *George Ivanovitch Gurdjieff, Man's Awakening and the Practice of Remembering Oneself*, Guild Press, 1968, p. 10.
13 D. T. Suzuki, *Essays in Zen Buddhism: First Series*, London, Luzac & Co., 1927, pp. 236, 285.

14 Translated from Charles Duits, 'Notes inédites'.
15 BT I, p. v.
16 ISM, p. 157.

3 The 'work' and its aim

1 ISM, p. 312.
2 ISM, p. 49.
3 ISM, p. 357.
4 ISM, p. 362.
5 ibid.
6 ISM, pp. 362–3.
7 Matthew 11: 25.
8 MWRM, p. 4.
9 MWRM, pp. 28–9.
10 ISM, p. 274.
11 ISM, p. 357.

4 Notes on *Beelzebub's Tales*

1 Translated from J. L. Borges, *Discussion*, Paris, Gallimard, 1966, pp. 19 ff.
2 ibid.
3 ibid.
4 BT I, pp. 122–3.
5 Translated from Charles Duits, 'Notes inédites'

5 Gurdjieff and 'word prostitution'

1 BT I, p. 3.
2 Translated from Manuel Rainoird, 'Belzébuth, un coup de maître', *Monde nouveau*, 104, October 1956, p. 54.
3 ibid., p. 55.
4 BT I, p. 14.
5 MWRM, p. 8.
6 MWRM, pp. 23–4.
7 Rainoird, op. cit., pp. 56, 57, 58.
8 Translated from J. L. Borges, *Discussion*, Paris, Gallimard, 1966, pp. 19 ff.

6 The myth of the 'organ Kundabuffer'

1 BT I, p. 81.
2 BT I, p. 82.
3 BT I, p. 84.

4 BT I, p. 86.
5 ibid.
6 BT I, p. 88.
7 BT I, pp. 88–9.
8 BT I, p. 89.
9 BT I, pp. 104–5.
10 BT III, p. 409.

7 'The Terror-of-the-Situation'

1 ISM, pp. 53–4.
2 P. D. Ouspensky, *The Psychology of Man's Possible Evolution*, London, Routledge & Kegan Paul, 1978.
3 ibid., pp. 10–11.
4 ISM, p. 14.
5 ISM, p. 55.
6 BT I, p. 394.
7 BT I, pp. 394–5.
8 BT III, p. 32.
9 BT I, p. 395.
10 BT I, p. 52.
11 BT I, p. 54.
12 BT I, p. 368.

8 The 'Very Saintly Labors' of Ashiata Shiemash

1 BT I, p. 353.
2 BT I, p. 356.
3 ibid.
4 BT I, pp. 357, 358.
5 BT I, pp. 357–8.
6 BT I, p. 362.
7 BT I, p. 363.
8 BT I, p. 351.
9 BT I, p. vii.
10 BT I, p. 361.
11 BT I, p. 359.
12 BT I, p. 370.
13 BT I, p. 372.
14 Translated from René Daumal, *L'Évidence absurde*, Paris, Gallimard, 1972, pp. 90, 91.
15 BT I, p. 372.
16 See ISM, pp. 57, 94.

17 BT I. p. 368.
18 BT I. pp. 367. 366.
19 BT I. p. 369.
20 BT I. p. 370.
21 BT I. p. 371.
22 BT I. p. 373.
23 BT I. p. 378.
24 BT I. p. 379.
25 BT I. p. 384.
26 BT I. p. 387.
27 BT I. pp. 385–6.

9 The destruction of the 'Very Saintly Labors'

1 BT I. p. 323.
2 BT I. p. 395.
3 ibid.
4 C. S. Nott. *Teachings of Gurdjieff: The Journal of a Pupil.* An account of Some Years With G. I. Gurdjieff and A. R. Orage in New York and Fontainebleau-Avon. London. Routledge & Kegan Paul. 1961. pp. 181. 183.
5 BT I. p. 397.
6 BT I. p. 399.
7 ibid.
8 BT I. p. 400.
9 BT I. p. 401.
10 ibid.
11 BT I. p. 398.
12 BT I. p. 402.
13 BT I. pp. 323. 324.
14 BT I. p. 329.
15 BT I. pp. 329. 330.
16 BT I. pp. 330–1.
17 BT I. p. 402.
18 BT I. p. 403.
19 BT I. p. 403.
20 BT I. p. 404.
21 ibid.

10 'Fruits of former civilizations'

1 BT II. p. 4.
2 ISM. p. 144.

3 ISM, p. 164.
4 BT II, pp. 7–13.
5 BT I, p. 386.
6 BT I, pp. 405–6.
7 BT I, p. 410.

11 The four 'bodies' of man

1 ISM, p. 65
2 ISM, p. 21.
3 ISM, p. 67.
4 ISM, p. 66.
5 ISM, p. 259.
6 ISM, p. 104.
7 ISM, p. 30.
8 ISM, pp. 36, 39.
9 ISM, p. 99.
10 ISM, p. 105.
11 ISM, p. 40.
12 ibid.
13 ISM, p. 41.
14 ISM, pp. 41–2.
15 ISM, p. 18.
16 ISM, p. 43.
17 ibid.
18 ISM, p. 44.
19 ISM, p. 93.

12 A true likeness of 'man' (extract from *Beelzebub's Tales*)

1 BT III, pp. 382–91.

13 Man's possible evolution

1 ISM, p. 70.
2 ISM, p. 68.
3 BT I, p. 15.
4 René Daumal, *A Night of Serious Drinking*, translated by David Coward and E. A. Lovatt, London, Routledge & Kegan Paul, 1979, pp. vii–viii.
5 ISM, p. 70.
6 ISM, p. 58.
7 ISM, p. 113.
8 ISM, p. 114.

9 ISM, p. 72.
10 Daumal, op. cit., p. 95.
11 ISM, p. 72.
12 ISM, p. 195.
13 ISM, p. 72.
14 ISM, p. 73.
15 ibid.
16 ibid.
17 ISM, p. 105.
18 ISM, pp. 109–10.
19 ISM, p. 110.
20 ISM, p. 147.
21 ISM, p. 150.
22 ISM, p. 153.
23 ISM, pp. 161, 162.
24 ISM, p. 163.
25 ISM, p. 8.
26 Translated from Charles Duits, 'Le pays de l'éclairement', in *Lettres nouvelles*, Paris, Denoël, 1967.
27 Translated from Duits, 'Dieu vert Ciguri', *Lettres nouvelles*, Jan. 1972.
28 ISM, p. 162.
29 ISM, p. 163.

14 The traditional ways and the way of the 'sly man'

1 ISM, p. 44.
2 ISM, p. 45.
3 ISM, p. 46.
4 ibid.
5 ibid.
6 ibid.
7 ibid.
8 ISM, p. 47.
9 ISM, p. 312.
10 ISM, p. 50.
11 ibid.
12 ISM, p. 49.
13 ISM, p. 50.
14 ISM, p. 312.
15 ISM, p. 202.
16 ISM, p. 203.
17 ISM, p. 201.
18 ibid.

19 ibid.
20 ISM, p. 199.
21 BT III, p. 398.
22 ISM, p. 199.
23 ISM, p. 200.
24 ISM, p. 204.
25 ISM, p. 202.
26 ISM, pp. 242–3.
27 ISM, p. 222.
28 ibid.
29 ISM, pp. 223–4.
30 ISM, p. 226.

15 The Law of Three

1 BT II, p. 51.
2 ISM, p. 75.
3 ISM, p. 77.
4 BT I, p. 138.
5 ISM, p. 77.
6 Maurice Nicoll, *Psychological Commentaries on the Teaching of G. I. Gurdjieff and P. D. Ouspensky*, London, Vincent Stuart & J. M. Watkins, 1952, vol. 1, p. 110.
7 ISM, pp. 78–9.
8 ISM, p. 76.
9 ISM, p. 80.
10 ISM, p. 84.
11 ISM, p. 83.

16 The Law of Seven

1 ISM, p. 122.
2 ISM, p. 123.
3 ibid.
4 ISM, p. 124.
5 ISM, p. 125.
6 ibid.
7 ISM, p. 126.
8 ISM, p. 127.
9 ISM, p. 129.
10 ISM, p. 132.
11 ISM, p. 138.
12 ISM, p. 134.

17   The lateral octave, the triple cosmic octave and the table of hydrogens

1 ISM. p. 25.
2 ISM. p. 135.
3 ISM. p. 169.
4 ibid.
5 ibid.
6 ISM. p. 170.
7 ibid.
8 ibid.
9 ISM. p. 171.
10 ISM. p. 172.
11 ISM. p. 175.

18   Man considered as a 'three-story factory'

1 ISM. p. 179.
2 ibid.
3 ISM. p. 180.
4 ISM. p. 181.
5 ibid.
6 ISM. p. 182.
7 ISM. p. 185.
8 ISM. p. 187.
9 ibid.
10 ISM. p. 188.
11 ibid.
12 ibid.
13 ISM. p. 193.
14 ibid.
15 ISM. p. 194.

19   The enneagram

1 ISM. p. 281.
2 ISM. p. 283.
3 ISM. p. 291.
4 ISM. p. 205.
5 ISM. p. 206.
6 ibid.
7 ISM. p. 293.
8 ISM. p. 294.
9 ibid.

20 Remarkable men and remarkable sayings

1 MWRM, p. 18.
2 MWRM, p. x.
3 Matthew 18: 3.
4 MWRM, p. 32.
5 MWRM, pp. 46–9, 55–7, 240–2.

Biological note

1 MWRM, p. 32.
2 ibid.
3 MWRM, p. 34.
4 MWRM, p. 40.
5 MWRM, p. 42.
6 BT I, p. 27.
7 BT I, p. 30.
8 BT I, pp. 34–5.
9 BT I, p. 35.
10 Translated from the editorial introduction to the French edition of MWRM, *Rencontres avec des hommes remarquables*, Paris, Editions Julliard, 1960, p. 12.
11 ISM, p. 4.
12 ISM, p. 7.
13 ISM, pp. 7–8.
14 Translated from Thomas de Hartman, *Notre vie avec Gurdjieff*, Paris, Planète, p. 26.
15 ibid., pp. 28, 29.
16 French edition of MWRM, p. 14.
17 ISM, p. 386.
18 BT I, p. 50.
19 French edition of MWRM, p. 14.
20 ibid., p. 15.
21 ibid., p. 14.
22 BT III, p. 374.
23 French edition of MWRM, p. 14.
24 BT III, p. 377.

Select bibliography

1 Basic texts

G. I. GURDJIEFF, *Beelzebub's Tales to His Grandson*, 3 vols, London, Routledge & Kegan Paul, 1976.
—— *Meetings With Remarkable Men*, London, Routledge & Kegan Paul, 1977.
P. D. OUSPENSKY, *In Search of the Miraculous: Fragments of an Unknown Teaching*, London, Routledge & Kegan Paul, 1977.
—— *The Fourth Way*, London, Routledge & Kegan Paul, 1972.
—— *A New Model of the Universe*, London, Routledge & Kegan Paul, 1938.
MAURICE NICOLL, *Psychological Commentaries on the Teaching of Gurdjieff and Ouspensky*, London, Vincent Stuart and J. M. Watkins.

2 Accounts and Studies

ANDERSON, MARGARET, *The Unknowable Gurdjieff*, London, Routledge & Kegan Paul, 1962.
DE HARTMANN, THOMAS, *Notre vie avec Gurdjieff*, Paris, Planète. *Our Life With Mr. Gurdjieff*, New York, Cooper Square, 1964.
HULME, KATHRYN, *Undiscovered Country*, Boston, Little Brown, 1966.
NOTT, C. S., *Teachings of Gurdjieff*, London, Routledge & Kegan Paul, 1961.
—— *Further Teachings of Gurdjieff*, London, Routledge & Kegan Paul, 1961.
PAUWELS, LOUIS, *Monsieur Gurdjieff*, Paris, Le Seuil.
PETERS, FRITZ, *Gurdjieff*, London, Wildwood House, 1976, containing:
—— *Boyhood With Gurdjieff*, New York, E. P. Dutton, 1964.
—— *Gurdjieff Remembered*, London, Gollancz, 1965.
WALKER, KENNETH, *A Study of Gurdjieff's Teaching*, London, Jonathan Cape, 1957.

ARKANA – NEW-AGE BOOKS FOR MIND, BODY AND SPIRIT

With over 150 titles currently in print, Arkana is the leading name in quality new-age books for mind, body and spirit. Arkana encompasses the spirituality of both East and West, ancient and new, in fiction and non-fiction. A vast range of interests is covered, including Psychology and Transformation, Health, Science and Mysticism, Women's Spirituality and Astrology.

If you would like a catalogue of Arkana books, please write to:

Arkana Marketing Department
Penguin Books Ltd
27 Wright's Lane
London W8 5TZ

ARKANA – NEW-AGE BOOKS FOR MIND, BODY AND SPIRIT

A selection of titles already published or in preparation

Encyclopedia of the Unexplained
Edited by Richard Cavendish Consultant: J. B. Rhine

'Will probably be the definitive work of its kind for a long time to come' – *Prediction*

The ultimate guide to the unknown, the esoteric and the unproven: richly illustrated, with almost 450 clear and lively entries from Alchemy, the Black Box and Crowley to faculty X, Yoga and the Zodiac.

Buddhist Civilization in Tibet Tulku Thondup Rinpoche

Unique among works in English, *Buddhist Civilization in Tibet* provides an astonishing wealth of information on the various strands of Tibetan religion and literature in a single compact volume, focusing predominantly on the four major schools of Buddhism: Nyingma, Kagyud, Sakya and Gelug.

The Living Earth Manual of Feng-Shui Stephen Skinner

The ancient Chinese art of Feng-Shui – tracking the hidden energy flow which runs through the earth in order to derive maximum benefit from being in the right place at the right time – can be applied equally to the siting and layout of cities, houses, tombs and even flats and bedsits; and can be practised as successfully in the West as in the East with the aid of this accessible manual.

In Search of the Miraculous: Fragments of an Unknown Teaching P. D. Ouspensky

Ouspensky's renowned, vivid and characteristically honest account of his work with Gurdjieff from 1915–18.

'Undoubtedly a *tour de force*. To put entirely new and very complex cosmology and psychology into fewer than 400 pages, and to do this with a simplicity and vividness that makes the book accessible to any educated reader, is in itself something of an achievement' – *The Times Literary Supplement*

ARKANA – NEW-AGE BOOKS FOR MIND, BODY AND SPIRIT

A selection of titles already published or in preparation

Head Off Stress: Beyond the Bottom Line D. E. Harding

Learning to head off stress takes no time at all and is impossible to forget – all it requires is that we dare take a fresh look at ourselves. This infallible and revolutionary guide from the author of *On Having No Head* – whose work C. S. Lewis described as 'highest genius' – shows how.

Shiatzu: Japanese Finger Pressure for Energy, Sexual Vitality and Relief from Tension and Pain
Yukiko Irwin with James Wagenvoord

The product of 4000 years of Oriental medicine and philosophy, Shiatzu is a Japanese variant of the Chinese practice of acupuncture. Fingers, thumbs and palms are applied to the 657 pressure points that the Chinese penetrate with gold and silver needles, aiming to maintain health, increase vitality and promote well-being.

The Magus of Strovolos: The Extraordinary World of a Spiritual Healer Kyriacos C. Markides

This vivid account introduces us to the rich and intricate world of Daskalos, the Magus of Strovolos – a true healer who draws upon a seemingly limitless mixture of esoteric teachings, psychology, reincarnation, demonology, cosmology and mysticism, from both East and West.

'This is a really marvellous book . . . one of the most extraordinary accounts of a "magical" personality since Ouspensky's account of Gurdjieff' – Colin Wilson

Meetings With Remarkable Men G. I. Gurdjieff

All that we know of the early life of Gurdjieff – one of the great spiritual masters of this century – is contained within these colourful and profound tales of adventure. The men who influenced his formative years had no claim to fame in the conventional sense; what made them remarkable was the consuming desire they all shared to understand the deepest mysteries of life.